When The Fire Fell

"I had a vision last Thursday morning. Here it is. Near me I could see a candle burning, and casting its light around. Far away in the distance, I could see a sun rising. And, Oh! what a sight it was. Not a winter nor an autumn sun, nor the sun of spring, but the sun of a summer's morn. Well, there was something divine in it. Its beams were like long arms, extending across the heavens. . . . Now, Syd, what is the meaning of this? . . . It is quite simple. Day is at hand. This is the beginning of a Revival. But, Oh! the great sun of the Revival is near at hand!"

Evan Roberts in a letter to Sidney Evans at the beginning of the Welsh Revival, November 5th, 1904

D1235369

When The Fire Fell

*The Great Welsh Revival of 1904
and Its Meaning For Revival Today*

R. Maurice Smith, B.A., M.A.

Preparedness Publications, Inc.
1280 Terminal Way, #3
Reno, Nevada 89502
Phone (702)333-5998/ FAX (702) 329-0852

All Scripture quotations from *The New American Standard Bible* (Copyright The Lockman Foundation, La Habra, California) unless otherwise indicated.

The Four Spiritual Laws courtesy of Campus Crusade For Christ International.

Cover Design by Jason Stuart, Spokane, Washington.

Ad Majorum Gloria Dei

Dedication

To The Memory Of

Dr. J. Edwin Orr

believer, evangelist, teacher, author
and keeper of the flame,
whose lectures on revival
first lit a fire and instilled a love of history and revival
in the heart of a young and impressionable college student

and

To The Memory of

Evan Roberts

the prophet and revivalist of Loughor,
whose heart I have come to understand,
and whose prayer bent a nation,
O Arglwydd, Plyg ni
(O Lord, Bend Us)

Table Of Contents

Prologue

"It is by revivals of religion that the Church of God makes its most visible advance. When all things seem becalmed, when no breath stirs the air, when the sea is like lead and the sky is low and gray, when all worship seems to have ended but the worship of matter, then it is that the Spirit of God is poured upon the Church, then it is that the Christianity of the Apostles and martyrs, not that of the philosophers and liberals, keeps rising . . . from the catacombs of oblivion, and appears young and fresh in the midst of the obsolete things of yesterday and the day before."

Sir William Robertson Nicoll
from *Princes of The Church*

Author's Preface

"A revival, therefore, is a work of grace effected by the Spirit of God on the souls of men . . . A revival presupposes the existence of real spiritual religion, as understood and taught by evangelical Christians."[1]

I was a senior at the University of North Carolina at Chapel Hill when I first encountered audio tapes of lectures by Dr. J. Edwin Orr on the history of revival. One lecture in particular had to do with a great revival in the tiny country of Wales in the years 1904-5.

I listened with amazement and rapt attention to story after story of how God poured out His Spirit upon person after person and church after church, until an entire nation was consumed. Young men had visions, old evangelists dreamed dreams of fruitful ministry, tens of thousands of converts confessed faith in Christ for the first time, back-slidden church members were gloriously renewed, churches were filled to over-flowing, sometimes around the clock, for 18 months. Judges were issued white gloves because crime had become almost non-existent and political rallies turned into prayer and praise meetings. It was a time of Divine visitation when, in the description of those who witnessed it, the fire of God fell and consumed everyone and everything in its path.

---

[1]Dr. George Smith, *History of Wesleyan Methodism*, 1862, quoted by J. Edwin Orr in *The Event of the Century*, published by International Awakening Press, P.O. Box 232, Wheaton, Illinois 60189.

15

Preface

What amazed me as much as the extent of God's blessing was the fact that I had never heard anything about it until then. After graduation I would serve two years on the staff of Campus Crusade For Christ before going on to Seminary. Again, during four years of Seminary, and more church history courses than I can remember, I never once heard about this remarkable out-pouring of God's Spirit in Wales. From the perspective of its importance in church history, not studying the Welsh Revival in the history of the 20th century church would be like studying the "secular" history of the 20th century and failing to mention World War II.

The Welsh Revival transformed Wales. But it also touched nearly every nation in the world, including every state in the United States. As revival swept over Wales with spontaneous prayer, increased crowds, personal conversions, confessions and quickenings, visitors flocked to Wales from every English speaking country, as well as from many non-English speaking countries. These people would then travel home and revival would break out in their footsteps. It was as if God was bringing them to Wales, setting them on fire and sending them out around the world as burning embers from which new fires would break forth. Spontaneous revival broke out in such divergent places as India, East Africa and Korea, often among missionaries who had visited Wales and *"received the fire"*.

Revival broke out in America in 1905 with such power and blessed fury that the General Assembly of the Presbyterian Church in The United States declared that *". . .*

in the judgment of many we have entered upon a great world-wide awakening . . . " The General Assembly minutes for 1905 are filled with reports of great revival sweeping churches, towns and states.

In Portland, Oregon, revival broke out with such power that more than 200 local department stores agreed in writing to close from 11:00 a.m. until 2:00 p.m. in order to allow their employees to attend prayer meetings.

The significance of the Welsh Revival lay in the fact that it was the starting point for the greatest worldwide outpouring of the Spirit of God in the twentieth century, touching virtually every continent (with the possible exception of Antarctica) and every nation of the world. In a sense, it was the match that God used to set fire to the world.

Unknown to most Christians today, this outpouring of the Holy Spirit, of which the Welsh Revival was only one expression, was the head-waters from which flowed the modern day Pentecostal, Charismatic and church renewal movements. Other than speaking in tongues (which broke out roughly two years after the revival) and manifestations of healings, nearly all of the current spiritual manifestations of the Charismatic movement were present in their early forms in the Welsh Revival. The Azusa Street meetings of 1906, to which most historians trace the modern origins of the Pentecostal/charismatic movements, were simply another of many powerful manifestations and expressions of this unprecedented outpouring of the Spirit of God, the after-effects of which continue on to our own day.

Preface

On a recent trip to England and Wales I was asked by an English pastor why the Welsh Revival disappeared so quickly. This is a common misconception which we will address in greater depth later. In reality, in many parts of the world, such as India, Africa, Korea, and China, the spreading flames of the Welsh Revival burned brightly for nearly a decade, up until the outbreak of World War I. It was the catastrophic blood-letting of World War I that brought this world wide revival to its conclusion.

The great Welsh Revival is now history, most of which has been overlooked and forgotten by the modern evangelical community. The purpose of this book is to suggest that we forget history at our own peril.

Indeed, the Church today runs several dangers with regard to revival. First, the Church runs the danger of forgetting what God has done in the past through revivals. The history of God's church during times of revival is a glorious time when, in the words of the Baptist Union of Wales, *"the Church has wakened and has put on the beautiful garments of her glory"*.

Second, the Church historian runs the danger of simply recording the fact that something happened and of endlessly critiquing the event until it dies the academic death of a thousand qualifications (see comments below on secular historiography).

Third, the Church runs the danger of expecting God to simply repeat, without change or variation, the same phenomena and experiences of the past. But God, while accomplishing the same timeless task of refreshing His Church for effective worship and ministry, is infinitely creative as He visits His Church afresh in each generation. And, as C.S. Lewis observed on numerous occasions, *He is not a tame lion.*

Finally, because the fires of genuine revival burn with unusual intensity, the danger lurks that the Church may use times of revival (and the associated manifestations) to determine its doctrine, rather than using its time tested biblical doctrine to test the spirits of revival.

I wish to suggest that there are important lessons for us today as we pray and ask God to renew His work in the midst of these years in which we live. What is the relationship of prayer and revival? What about the role of music and singing? Which comes first, spirit filled worship or revival? What about the role of conviction and confession of sin, the manifestation of gifts, laughter, and the troublesome "excesses" which seem to attend outbreaks of great revival?

Today we sing wonderful choruses which declare *"What a mighty God we serve."* But the history of the great Welsh Revival of 1904 suggests that we today have not yet seen what God can truly do in a person, a church and a nation when He sovereignly chooses to pour out His Divine fire of revival in response to the earnest prayers of His people. The great Welsh Revival of 1904-1905 was like a demonstration of what God can do when He sends times of refreshing to His church.

Preface

In many ways the coming of revival is like the coming of Spring. When the new life of Spring comes to the tree, the new life bursts forth in the old branches. And branches that seemed dead during the long winter months suddenly burst forth with the glorious new life. But if any of the old branches resist the new life, the new life is powerful enough to break forth in new buds and new branches. It will not be held back.

My wife and I live on a river below a small flood control and hydroelectric dam. One day upon arriving home I discovered that the water level in the river had dropped to the lowest level we had ever seen. It felt like the life had left the river. A few hours later, while doing yard work I heard a strange noise. After a brief pause I realized what it was. The river had returned in all of its fullness and was flowing again with life. Then, within only a few weeks, the river had risen to its highest level in over twenty years!

So it is with revival. Just when we think that all of the life has run out of the Church, God opens the flood gates of His Spirit and suddenly the river of life is again flowing through the church in all of its fullness and power, sweeping all things before it, to the joy of many, the consternation of a few, and the surprise of all.

A word is in order about the nature and intent of this book. It is first and foremost a history of God's real time dealings in the nation of Wales leading up to and during the years of 1904 - 1906. Modern secular historians have a difficult time comprehending that there are forces outside of the historical continuum which affect, even determine, historical events.

Richard Riss, mirroring the thinking of the late Dr. Francis A. Schaeffer, has observed that this is due to the decline and loss of a Christian consensus. People today, and particularly academics and historians, regard themselves as too sophisticated to assign Divine purposes to natural or historical events. [2]

The Great Welsh Revival of 1904 is an historical fact. But the secular historian observing and reporting upon it might want to delve into such things as the sociological milieu, the economic conditions and political trends of the time period in order to attribute the outbreak of "religious fervor" to one or a combination of these causes. Only in this way can secular historians come to an academically acceptable "understanding" of the origins of revival. This approach says much about the spiritual sterility of modern historiography [3] (at whose altar even many aspiring Christian historians are obliged to present offerings in order to acquire their mantle of academic respectability - called a "degree"). Dr. J. Edwin Orr, who possessed three earned doctoral

---

[2] Richard M. Riss, *A Survey of 20-th Century Revival Movements In North America* (Hendrickson Publishers, Inc.: Peabody, 1988), p. 3.

[3] By the term "historiography" I am referring to a philosophy of history. Perhaps the best contemporary critique of the modern secular historiography has been written by Herbert Schlossberg in Chapter 1 of his excellent work *Idols For Destruction: The Conflict of Christian Faith and American Culture* (Crossway Books: Wheaton, 1990).

Preface

degrees, was sometimes accused of being less than thoroughly analytical in his evaluation of the history of revival. This criticism seems to smack of a secular historiography which would subject all revivals to the death of a thousand cultural explanations.

Let us be clear from the outset about the origin of "revival." As discussed in this book revival is defined as an out-pouring of the Spirit of God at a time and upon a people of God's own sovereign choosing, resulting in the spiritual renewal of believers and the evangelization of unbelievers. And as the Spirit of God is like the wind which *"blows where it wishes and you hear the sound of it, but do not know where it comes from and where it is going"* (John 3:8), so too, genuine revival is experienced but never explained, described by men but never determined by them, prayed for and yearned for, but never planned for by the hand and purpose of man. If this definition is not sufficiently analytical for the post-modern historians of today I can only state that, all things considered, I would rather be spiritually revived by the Spirit of God than historically analyzed by a modern academic.

Finally, I am deeply indebted to the late Dr. J. Edwin Orr, whose life and ministry was dedicated to documenting the history of revivals around the world. I first became aware of Dr. Orr's ministry through audio tapes of his lectures to the staff of Campus Crusade for Christ, particularly those lectures at Purdue University during the summer of 1973. Campus Crusade had the foresight to record those lectures on audio tapes which are now available as a ten-part series entitled *"Spiritual Awakenings of the 20th Century"* by contacting the audio tape ministry of Campus Crusade at 1-800-729-4351. While Dr. Orr was a prodigious writer on the topic of revival many of his books have fallen out of print at this time, as have most books on the great Welsh Revival of 1904. The reader will find a select bibliography at the end of this book.

There is much talk and prayer about the need for revival as we approach the end of this decade and the beginning of the new millennium. This modest book is offered as an encouragement to all those who hunger for another great outpouring of the Spirit of God upon His Church in the heartfelt prayer that what He has done before He will do again in our day. May we sing with earnestness:

Flow O mighty holy river,
Flow in measure
Great and strong;
Hold not back
Thy generous blessing,
Flood this desert
With Thy song.

Parched and arid,
Hear the crying
Of Thy barren
Broken Church;
Bring Revival to the dying,
Quench the aching
Of their thirst.

Preface

Once Again
Release Thy floodgate,
Shower Heaven's fruitful touch;
Till the earth
Appeased, rejoicing ,
Rings the message of Thy love.

Flow O mighty holy river,
Flow in measure
Great and strong;
Hold not back
Thy generous blessing,
Flood this desert
With Thy song [4]

Introduction

*"When God intends great mercy for His people,
he first sets them a'praying."*
Matthew Henry

"Before I go hence . . ."

In the year that D. L. Moody died (1899), at the end of a long and fruitful ministry of evangelism, he declared, *"Now the question is shall we have a great and mighty harvest or shall we go on discussing our differences? As far as I am concerned, I am terribly tired of it, and I would like before I go hence to see the whole church of God quickened as it was in (18)57, and a wave going from Maine to California that shall sweep thousands into the kingdom of God. Why not?."*

The forerunner of **Moody** magazine (called **The Institute Tie**) said in 1906, *"His desire was not gratified in the flesh, but the revival has come."* [5] It is no secret that in 1898-1899 prayer meetings were begun at Moody Bible Institute for a new awakening. But what was it about 1857 that so enthralled Moody that the great evangelist, who had witnessed so much of God's blessing, would wistfully pray for a repetition of that year? And what was it about the year 1906 that led **Moody** magazine to declare that the evangelist's prayer had been answered?

---

[5] **The Institute Tie**, Chicago, Moody Bible Institute, April, 1906, page 277. My thanks to Janet McVay of **Moody** magazine for her invaluable assistance in hunting down this quote. In March of 1905 **The Institute Tie** ran a four page article on the Welsh Revival. See March, 1905, pages 305 - 308.

Introduction

Longing For Revival

To the great surprise of many, the answer can be readily found in the *Minutes of the General Assembly of the Presbyterian Church (USA)*. In the *Annual Narrative of the State of Religion* contained in the minutes for the year 1857 there appeared a section entitled *"Longing For Revival"*. Listen to what the author writes for that year:

"Another and the last evidence, that we cite, of an increasing vigor and efficiency in our denomination is, the intense longing, breathed through all the Narratives for a general, glorious outpouring of the Spirit. The past year has not been one which may be characterized as a year of revivals, although many churches in many Presbyteries have been greatly quickened, and some have been favored with spiritual influences of extraordinary power. . . . This longing for revivals we cannot but consider a cheering indication of the noblest life. Next to a state of actual revival is the sense of its need, and the struggle to attain it at any sacrifice of treasure, toil or time. We trust that the period is not distant, when this state of actual, general, glorious revival shall be ours. . ." [6]

For the Presbyterian Church, 1857 was a year of great longing for revival, with noticeable outbreaks of revival which were the down payment and promise of more to come. These were only the first showers of a coming storm.

---

[6] ***Minutes of the General Assembly of the Presbyterian Church in the United States of America with an Appendix***, 1857, page 418.

Introduction

The Breaking Storm

The anticipated storm broke in all its fury and blessing in 1858. In the *Minutes of the General Assembly* for 1858, a new section appeared entitled *"Great Awakening"*. Longing had turned into realization.

"The closing sentiment in the Narrative of this last year, was the desire, expressed by several of our Presbyteries, for the revival of God's work. The cheering intelligence which now reaches us from every part of the land, is the realization of this desire. . . . The meeting of the present Assembly occurs in the midst of what has been very properly styled "The Great Awakening". . . . This wave of blessing is rolling over the land. Already it has reached every Presbytery within our bounds" [7]

"How Often Shall I Pray?"

The precise beginnings of the 1857 awakening are difficult to pin down, but there is little doubt that the Fulton Street Prayer Meeting played a pivotal role. In 1857 a New York businessman named Jeremiah Lanphier, a lay missionary with the North Dutch Reformed Church, developed a concern for businessmen in the Manhattan area. He asked for and received permission to open the doors of the North Dutch Church on the corner of Fulton and William Streets from 12 Noon till 1:00 p.m. for prayer one day every

---

[7] *Minutes of the General Assembly of the Presbyterian Church in the United States of America with an Appendix*, 1858, page 610 - 611.

week. Lanphier then wrote and distributed a small handbill entitled *"How Often Shall I Pray?"* which invited businessmen to come and pray. It declared, *"This meeting is intended to give merchants, mechanics, clerks, strangers and businessmen generally an opportunity to stop and call on God amid the perplexities incident to their respective avocations."*[8]

At the first meeting on September 23, 1857 six men showed up. At the second meeting on October 1st there were 20 men in attendance. On October 7th between thirty and forty men came for prayer. So encouraging was the response that a decision was made to open the church for prayer daily instead of weekly. On October 8th the room was filled. By October 14th over 100 men attended *"many of them not professors of religion but under conviction of sin and seeking an interest in Christ."*[9]

By the beginning of December other churches began opening their doors during the day for prayer, the purpose being *"intercession for the Spirit's outpouring."* J. Edwin Orr points out that many business men gave these prayer meetings a first place in their lives with a marvelous result. One man, visiting New York to purchase goods, was busy selecting items when the noon hour arrived. He asked the

---

[8] Quoted by J. Edwin Orr, *The Event Of The Century: The 1857 - 1858 Awakening* (International Awakening Press: Wheaton, 1989), page 54.

[9] Ibid.

wholesaler to work through the noon hour so that he could catch the evening river-boat home. The wholesaler responded, *"No! I can't help that. I have something to attend that is of more importance than the selling of goods. I must attend the noon-day prayer meeting. It will close at one o'clock, and I will then fill out your order."* Both men proceeded to the noonday meeting. At the meeting the visitor was so impressed and moved that he became a Christian. Upon his return to Albany he immediately started up a noonday prayer meeting there.[10] The fire of revival had begun to spread.

"Till Every Knee Is Bowed"

By the end of 1857 the fires of revival were already burning in many parts of the United States, including Chicago, Illinois. In 1856 a young businessman had moved to Chicago. Shortly after his arrival he rented a pew (yes, in those days church pews could be rented and reserved!) in the Plymouth Congregational Church and began persuading young men to go with him to church and fill his rented pew. In 1857 he approached the church leadership and asked if he might be allowed to teach a Sunday School class. They informed him that they already had more teachers than students, but he could teach a class if he could bring in enough students to fill it himself. Sure enough, he showed up the following Sunday with seventeen street urchins in tow. During the awakening he wrote home to his mother in New England, describing the blessing of those days, *". . . I go to meeting every night, and oh how I enjoy it. It seems as if God*

---

[10] Ibid., page 55-56.

were here Himself. Mother, pray for me. Pray that this work may go on, till every knee is bowed." [11]

The awakening of 1857 -1858 was a time of great blessing for this young businessman. He was so successful at "drumming up" Sunday School students among the street urchins of Chicago that he rented an abandoned saloon building where he soon had between 1,000 and 1,500 students enrolled. This abandoned saloon became the largest Sunday School in Chicago. All the while, he had remained active in his business as a salesman. But by 1860 he chose to resign his $5,000 per year business to "live by faith" and labor full time in the on-going revival. In the year of his death, Dwight Lyman Moody would pray to see once again such a great outpouring of the Spirit of God and such a quickening of the Church as he had seen at the beginning of his ministry in 1857. His prayer would be answered five years after his death in the great Welsh Revival of 1904.

---

[11] Ibid., page 134.

Chapter 1
Longing And Preparation

Longing in Wales

Wales, a small but beautiful country on the southwest coast of Great Britain, has been called *"the land of periodic revivals."* Between 1762 and 1862 (from the time of the "first Great Awakening" until the time of the "second Great Awakening") Wales experienced no less than fifteen outstanding revivals. The revivals encompassing the period of the "first Great Awakening" of the 1700s gave to Wales the Calvinistic Methodist Church and its wonderful hymnology. It became a singing church.

The "second Great Awakening" of 1859-1862 gave Wales its theology. David Morgan, a minister of the Calvinistic Methodist (Presbyterian) Church of Wales, was greatly used of God during this remarkable outpouring of the Spirit of God when an estimated 110,000 souls were added to the churches of Wales.

Additional revivals in the last half of the 19th century contributed to Wales reputation as the land of revivals. In particular, the ministry of Richard Owens in North Wales in the early 1880s was greatly blessed with some 13,000 souls won for Christ under his personal ministry. When he died at the young age of forty-eight, "Richard Owen, the Revivalist" was a household name throughout Wales.

But like yesterday's manna, yesterday's spiritual renewals were insufficient food for the Church. By the end of

Chapter 1 - Longing And Preparation

the nineteenth century the spiritual condition of the churches in Wales was on the decline. The effects of the 1859 revival (yes, the Welsh counterpart of the 1857 - 1858 awakening in America!) had worn off, except in the memories of old evangelists and pastors who, like D. L. Moody, longed and prayed for another such time. [12]

Church membership in Wales had declined in the decade of the 1890s, with the North Wales Association of the Calvinistic Methodists (the Presbyterian Church in Wales) reporting a loss of 12,844 for the year 1899 alone. Sunday services were poorly attended in both Non-conformist churches and the Anglican Church in Wales. The declines were generally acknowledged and universally deplored. The question confronting the church was how to combat worldliness in the pew and powerlessness in the pulpit.

And yet there was a hunger for God among groups of believers and leaders in the Church which was laying the foundation for a spiritual awakening. Prayer meetings were being held worldwide for a revival in the new century.

In 1898-1899 there were all-night prayer meetings held at Moody Bible Institute for revival. The same was true world-wide in such diverse places as India and Korea. Ten

---

[12] There is an excellent book entitled *"The Welsh Revival: Its Origin And Development"*, by Thomas Phillips. It is an eyewitness account of the 1859 revival. It is available from Banner of Truth at 3 Murrayfield road, Edinburgh EH12 6EL, England, or P.O. Box 621, Carlisle, Pennsylvania 17013, USA

thousand people were enrolled in prayer cells in Melbourne, Australia.

In the winter of 1900 the Methodists were reporting an increasing number of conversions in evangelistic campaigns throughout the U.S.A. They announced the Methodist Forward Movement. They raised $20 million and planned to win two million souls to Christ. They stated in an editorial, *"It was believed that with better knowledge of how to work and a feeling that it was a Church-wide movement, a great religious awakening might be secured at the opening of the twentieth century."* [13] One Methodist commented later that *"God waited until we got our project out of the way, then shortly afterwards He sent the revival."* [14]

James A. Stewart, the great Scottish evangelist and author of *"A Man In Christ,"* estimated that there were at least forty thousand earnest believers seeking God in prayer for revival before 1904. By 1905 the prayed-for revival was underway.

In 1902 Dean David Howell of Wales declared, *"Take notice! If it were known that this is my last message to my*

---

[13] Editorial, *Western Christian Advocate*, July 4, 1900, quoted by J. Edwin Orr, *The Flaming Tongue: The Impact of Twentieth Century Revivals* (Moody Press: Chicago, 1973), p 66.

[14] J. Edwin Orr, *"1981 Prayer Series,"* No. 1, *"Prayer And Revival "* Copyright 1994 Campus Crusade For Christ, International, Audio Tape Series available from Integrated Resources, the audio tape ministry of Campus Crusade for Christ International (800)729-4351.

Chapter 1 - Longing And Preparation

fellow countrymen before being summoned to judgment, the chief need of my country and my dear nation at present is a spiritual revival through the outpouring of the Holy Spirit. "[15] Howell was summoned to judgment only one month later, two years before his longings were to be answered in the outbreak of the greatest revival Wales had ever known.

But the churches of Wales were not blind to their own need. According to London journalist W.T. Stead, there was a growing sense longing and burden of prayer for revival:

"For a long time past the Welsh Christians had been moved to pray specifically for the quickening of religious life in their midst. The impulse appears to have been sporadic and spontaneous. In remote country hamlets, in mining villages buried in distant valleys, one man or one woman would have it laid upon his or her soul to pray that the Holy Spirit might be poured out upon the cause in which they were spiritually concerned. There does not seem to have been much organized effort. It was all individual, local, and strictly limited to the neighborhood. But prayer circles formed by devout persons who agree to unite together in prayer at a given hour every day have long been a recognized form of prevailing prayer. By these circles there are some 30,000 or 40,000 people now banded together to pray for a world-wide Revival. All this was general. It was preparing the way. A great longing for

---

[15] *Y Cyfaill Eglwsig*, December, 1902; cf *Missionary Review of the World*, 1905, pp. 163 ff, quoted by Orr, *The Flaming Tongue: The Impact of Twentieth Century Revivals* (Moody Press: Chicago, 1973), page 1.

Chapter 1 - Longing And Preparation

Revival was abroad in the land. The Churches were conscious that there was something in the air. " [16]

Keswick Conventions

Keswick Conventions were conferences, English in origin, which were intended to promote the deepening of the spiritual life. In the early 1900s a number of Welsh church leaders were praying for the beginning of Keswick Conventions in Wales. Welsh church leaders invited noted Keswick speaker Dr. F.B. Meyers to minister to them in Keswick-style conventions at the beautiful Welsh spa in Llandrindod Wells. The conference was well attended by young Welsh pastors who were greatly blessed as they devoted themselves to prayer for an awakening in Wales.

Several noted pastors were greatly touched at the Llandrindod conference and began traveling widely, conducting missions for the deepening of the spiritual life. Later, when the Welsh Revival was well underway many Keswick leaders would claim that the revival could be traced directly to the effect of the Keswick conferences.[17]

---

[16] W.T. Stead, *The Revival In The West*, page 57, in *The Revival of 1905* (London: "The Review of Reviews" Publishing Office, 1905).

[17] Jessie Penn-Lewis, a leader in the Welsh Keswick movement was instrumental in advancing this claim through her book *The Awakening In Wales*, written during the heat of the revival. She called the Keswick movement "the hidden springs" of the revival.

Chapter 1 - Longing And Preparation

"Mary, Are You Saved?"

In the years leading up to 1904 Wales was criss-crossed by a number of able and dedicated evangelists. The Reverend John Pugh had begun an evangelistic ministry in the Calvinistic Methodist Church of Wales (later known as the Presbyterian Church of Wales) in the 1870s. It later became known as the Forward Movement and stressed open-air evangelism. When Pugh moved to Cardiff, the capital of Wales, in 1891, he met Seth Joshua who had been converted in a Salvation Army meeting. Together, the evangelistic work of John Pugh and Seth Joshua covered most of South Wales.

Seth Joshua was known for being both forthright and studious. His wife related the following story as an example of his forthrightness: *"One day he turned to me, and asked, 'Mary, are you saved?' Surprised at such a question I said, 'Well, you know, Seth, that I have been confirmed'. 'Yes, my dear,' he added, 'and vaccinated; but are you saved?'"*[18] Seth Joshua's forthrightness would serve him well when the revival began in earnest.

"What Does Jesus Christ Mean To You?"

At the outset of the Welsh Revival Joseph Jenkins was the   pastor of New Quay (pronounced "key") Church in

---

[18]Eifion Evans, *The Welsh Revival Of 1904*, Evangelical Press, 1969, 136 Rosendale Road, London SE 21 or Box 2453, Grand Rapids, Michigan 49501, page 53.

Cardiganshire. He was deeply concerned about the spiritual state of the young people in his church and had begun spending prolonged times in prayer for them. He was concerned that his youth group had become more social than Christian. One Sunday morning in February of 1904 he challenged the 60 youths in his Christian Endeavour movement. *"What does Jesus Christ mean to you?"* he asked. The question was embarrassing to them. There was a prolonged silence. One boy eventually spoke up and said, *"Jesus Christ is the hope of the world."* Jenkins responded, *"Never mind the world. What does Jesus Christ mean to you?"* Finally, young Florie Evans, who had been converted by Jenkins only two weeks before, testified to the cold youth meeting, *"I love the Lord Jesus with all my heart."* This simple statement of personal faith deeply moved the Christian Endeavour movement. The effect was startling, and resulted in an overpowering sense of God's presence in the church. The fire of revival had been lit. The young people soon began visiting other local churches carrying the fire and sharing the blessing.

"Please God, Give Me Wales"

In the 1970s a retired Presbyterian minister lived in Port Hueneme in California. His name was Dr. Peter Joshua. He was the son of Seth Joshua (born April 10,1859). By 1904 Seth Joshua was an official evangelist of the Welsh Presbyterian Church, then called the Calvinistic Methodist Church. Along with John Pugh, Seth Joshua was also an official evangelist for the Forward Movement in Wales. He began to pray a most unusual prayer. He was concerned with the over-emphasis of the Presbyterian church upon the academic and educational qualifications rather than the spiritual qualifications of its ministers. So he had begun to ask God to raise up a lad from the mines or fields of Wales (even as He had taken Elisha from behind the plough), not from Cambridge or Oxford to pander to the people's pride, but a lad from the mines or the fields to revive his people and lead them back to God. He could scarcely have imagined that God would use his own ministry to anoint the very person who would fulfill this prayer!

Years later Dr. Peter Joshua told a story about missing ("mitching") school one day and going to a local park to play. Suddenly he spotted his father walking in the park. Hiding in some bushes he watched as his father walked by:

"As he came near I was frightened as I heard that he was crying (something I thought never my Dad would ever do) and as he went by he was saying, 'Please God, give me Wales', and kept saying this as long as I could hear him. After a while I ran back home, and while I had to explain to mother that I had mitched school, I asked her what was wrong with Dad, and told her that I had heard him crying and saying 'Give me Wales.' She ruffled her hair and said, 'You'll understand one day.' God never gave Wales to my Dad, although he gave him many souls, but one day when he was preaching when he made an appeal Evan Roberts was the only one who stood to his feet and trusted the Saviour. God never gave Wales to my Dad, but he gave Wales to Evan

Roberts. " [19]

Fire In New Quay

In September of 1904 Seth Joshua went to New Quay to visit Jenkins' church. To his surprise he found a real congregational awakening going on. He could not know at the time that He was witnessing the beginning of the greatest revival Wales had ever known. He wrote in his diary:[20]

(Sunday, 18th September) "I have never seen the power of the Holy Spirit so powerfully manifested among the people as at this place just now . . . It was easy to preach today."

(Monday, 19th) "Revival is breaking out here in greater power. Many souls are receiving full assurance of salvation. The spirit of prayer and of testimony is falling in a marvelous manner. The young are receiving the greatest measure of blessing. They break out into prayer, praise, testimony and exhortation in a wonderful way."

---

[19] This anecdote is related in a letter in the possession of Mr. Meurig Thomas of Llangeler, Dyfed. A copy is in the Evangelical Library of Wales at Bridgend, quoted by Brynmor P. Jones, *Voices From The Welsh Revival 1904-1905* (Evangelical Press of Wales: Bridgend, 1995), page 16.

[20] Evans, *The Welsh Revival of 1904*, Page 59-60. Seth Joshua's original diaries, written in Welsh, are today located in the official archives of the Calvinistic Methodist Church, National Library of Wales, in Aberystwyth, Cardiganshire, Wales.

Chapter 1 - Longing And Preparation

(Tuesday, 20th) "The revival goes on. I cannot leave the building . . . until 12 and even 1 o'clock in the morning. I have closed the service several times and yet it would break out again quite beyond control of human power."

(Friday, 23rd) "I am of the opinion that forty conversions took place this week. It is as near as I can fix it. I also think that those seeking assurance may be fairly counted as converts, for they had never received Jesus as a personal saviour before . . . I shall thank God for this blessed time to my own soul. I am saturated, melted and made soft as willing clay in the hands of a potter."

Seth Joshua had an unparalleled week of blessing. He next went to visit Newcastle Emlyn college. This was a training college for the Presbyterian Ministry, but it was not a place on fire for Christ. Seth Joshua spoke to the students for a week, telling them about the revival which was breaking out at New Quay.

He preached 4 times on Sunday the 25th of September, and afterwards wrote *"nothing has moved yet."* He spoke again on Monday, the 26th. Afterwards he wrote, *"I find scarcely a soul here in the joy of assurance. It is a pitiable sight to me. When I tested the meeting only a small handful among hundreds would stand up to confess a present salvation. The witness of the church is nothing in this state."*[21]

But Seth Joshua's discouragement was short-lived. On

---

[21] Ibid., page 61.

Tuesday, the 28th, a remarkable thing happened. Fifteen of the youth from New Quay came and spoke to the students at Newcastle Emlyn. They brought with them "the fire". Seth Joshua later recorded, *"I did not preach but allowed them to speak, pray, sing and exhort as the Holy Spirit led them. The fire burned all before it. Souls were melted and many cried out for salvation."* [22]

Evan Roberts

During this week Seth Joshua ministered at a meeting where a young man by the name of Evan Roberts was present. Roberts was 26 years of age and a former coal miner (a "collier"). Born on July 8, 1878 of a devout Welsh Calvinistic Methodist family, Roberts had always had a great passion for revival. He had been a devoted christian for many years. He had offered himself for the ministry in 1903 and after an extraordinary mystical experience was in the habit of awaking nightly at 1 a.m. for communion with God. Evan Roberts had been praying for revival. He had told one of his friends, *"For ten or eleven years I have prayed for a revival. I could sit up all night to read or talk about revival. It was the Spirit that moved me to think about a revival."* [23]

---

[22] Ibid.

[23] **Western Mail,** *The Religious Revival in Wales,* Consolidated reports consisting of six pamphlets of collected newspaper reports issued in 1904-1905, iii, page 31, quoted by Evans, *The Welsh Revival of 1904,* page 64.

Chapter 1 - Longing And Preparation

While working as a collier (coal miner) Roberts was once in an explosion when a page of his beloved Bible was scorched by the explosion. At the time it was open to 2 Chronicles 6 where Solomon prayed for a revival. The page was permanently scorched by the explosive tongue of fire. When Roberts later became world renown during the revival, a picture of this Bible went around the world.[24]

Evan Roberts was recovering from a cold and was unable to hear Seth Joshua until Tuesday night. When he heard Seth Joshua speak about the revival currently going on in the New Quay congregation, he felt that the time had come. Evan Roberts and several of the students at New Castle Emlyn petitioned the principal of the college to be allowed to attend meetings at nearby Blaenannerch, 8 miles away, at which Seth Joshua and Joseph Jenkins would be speaking. Principal Evan Phillips agreed and they were given permission to go to the meetings.

"O Lord, Bend Us"

On Thursday, September 29th, Evan Roberts and some twenty students started out at 6:00 a.m. to attend a 7 a.m. meeting at the Blaenannerch conference. As they broke for breakfast, Seth Joshua concluded his preaching with a

---

[24] David Matthews, *I Saw The Welsh Revival* (Moody Press: Chicago, 1951), page 14. Stead also records this event in *The Revival In The West*, page 42.

prayer in Welsh, *"O Arglwydd, plyg ni" "O Lord, bend us"*.
[25] Evan Roberts was deeply and visibly moved by this prayer.
According to Roberts, *" 'That is what you stand in need of,'
said the Spirit to me. And Oh! In going through the door I
prayed within myself, 'Oh! Lord, bend us.' "*[26]

He refused to eat breakfast. On the way into the 9
o'clock meeting Seth Joshua commented, *"We are going to
have a wonderful meeting here to-day,"* to which Roberts
replied *"I am just bursting."* When the meeting resumed at 9
a.m., Roberts knew he must pray. As he waited for others to
finish praying he said , *"I felt some living energy or force
entering my bosom. It took my breath away, and my legs
trembled exceedingly."* Evan Roberts recounted the event
himself, *"I fell on my knees with my arms on the seat before
me, the perspiration poured down my face and my tears
streamed quickly - until I thought that the blood came out.
Soon Mrs. Davies, Mona, New Quay, came to wipe my
perspiration. . . It was awful on me for about two minutes. I
cried 'Bend me, bend me, bend me; Oh! Oh! Oh! Oh! Oh!
When wiping my perspiration Mrs. Davies said, 'Oh
wonderful grace!' 'Yes,' said I, 'Oh wonderful grace!' It was
God commending His love that bent me, and I not seeing
anything in Him to commend. After I was bent, a wave of*

---

[25] The word "bend" in Welsh ("plyg") is much stronger than in
English. The Welsh word carries the sense of to bend, mold or shape, like
the potter shapes the clay.

[26] D. M. Phillips, **Evan Roberts, The Great Welsh Revivalist
And His Work** (London: Marshall Brothers, 1906), page 124.

peace filled my bosom. When I was in this feeling the audience sang heartily, 'I am coming, coming, Lord, to Thee!' What came to my mind after this was, the bending in the day of judgment. Then I was filled with sympathy for the people who will have to bend in the judgment day, and I wept. Afterwards, the salvation of souls weighed heavily upon me.[27] Seth Joshua wrote in his diary, *"One young man was deeply moved"*. Indeed he was. Evan Roberts would always remember this day as *"Blaenanerch's great meeting."*

That was the crisis experience of Evan Roberts. When his burden lifted Roberts rose from prayer a changed man, *"I felt ablaze with a desire to go through the length and breadth of Wales to tell of the Saviour; and had it been possible, I was willing to pay God for doing so."* [28]

"A Particle Of Radium In Our Midst"

Roberts returned to Newcastle Emlyn College, but could hardly bring himself to concentrate on his studies. He and his roommate, Sydney Evans, spent much time praying and reading together. Roberts began to form a team of students to travel and preach throughout Wales (he even took $1,000 from his personal savings to finance the team) .

One midnight, after Roberts had been walking in the garden in communion with God, he went indoors, his face

---

[27] Ibid., page 124-125.

[28] Ibid., page 125

shining to the point of glowing. Sidney Evans (who later married Evan Roberts sister and went on to India as a missionary) was astonished and asked, *"Evan, what has happened to you?" "Oh, Syd,"* he replied, *"I had a vision of all Wales being lifted up to heaven. We are going to see the mightiest revival that Wales has ever known - and the Holy Spirit is coming soon, so we must get ready."* [29] Roberts then asked Sydney Evans directly, with a piercing look in his eyes that Sidney Evans never forgot, *"Sidney, do you believe God could give us a hundred thousand souls?".*[30]

The vision of 100,000 souls being won to Christ was a recurring theme for Roberts. At one time he recorded a vision of an arm and hand holding out piece of paper with the number *100,000* written on it. From that time onward, whenever he prayed, Roberts had no peace of spirit until he had asked God specifically for that number of souls.[31] Amazingly, the official church records show that within 6 months God had indeed brought no less than 100,000 souls into the fellowship of His Church.

These were exciting days, and the two men found it difficult to concentrate on their Greek studies. Principal Evan Phillips, himself a child of the 1859 revival, described these

---

[29] Colin Whittaker, *Great Revivals* (Radiant Books: Springfield, 1984) page 107.

[30] Orr, *The Flaming Tongue*, page 6.

[31] Evans, *The Welsh Revival of 1904*, page 79.

days, *"Evan Roberts was like a particle of radium in our midst. Its fire was consuming and felt abroad as something which took away sleep, cleared the channels of tears, and sped the golden wheels of prayer throughout the area . . . I did not weep much in the 1859 revival, but I have wept now until my heart is supple. In the midst of the greatest tearfulness I have found the greatest joy. I had felt for a year or two that there was a sighing in the wind, and something whispered that the storm could not be far away. Soon I felt the waters to begin to cascade. Now the bed belongs to the river and Wales belongs to Christ."*[32]

The embers of revival fire were now aglow, fanned by the breath of God. It was only a matter of time before they would burst forth in unquenchable fire.

---

[32] Evans, *The Welsh Revival of 1904*, page 72.

Chapter 2
And The Fire Fell

Great God of wonders! All Thy ways
Are matchless, godlike, and divine;
But the fair glories of Thy grace
More godlike and unrivall'd shine:
Who is a pardoning God like Thee?
Or who has grace so rich and free?

In wonder lost, with trembling joy,
We take the pardon of our God,
Pardon for crimes of deepest dye;
A pardon bought with Jesu's blood.
Who is a pardoning God like Thee?
Or who has grace so rich and free?

O may this strange, this matchless grace,
This godlike miracle of love,
Fill the wide earth with grateful praise,
And all the angelic choirs above:
Who is a pardoning God like Thee?
Who has grace so rich and free?

Evan Roberts' Favorite Hymn
Translated by The Reverend Joseph Harris[33]

"I have A Word For You From God"

Sidney Evans and Evan Roberts found it increasingly

---

[33]Phillips, *Evan Roberts*, n.p.

hard to concentrate on their studies. Their burden was for the saving of souls. One Sunday evening in October Roberts had a vision that would determine his future course.

"And one Sunday, as I sat in the chapel, I could not fix my mind upon the service, for always before my eyes I saw, as in a vision, the schoolroom in my own village. And there, sitting in rows before me, I saw my old companions and all the young people, and I saw myself addressing them. I shook my head impatiently, and strove to drive away this vision, but it always came back. And I heard a voice in my inward ear as plain as anything, saying, 'Go and speak to these people.' And for a long time I would not. But the pressure became greater and greater, and I could hear nothing of the sermon. Then at last I could resist no longer, and I said, 'Well, Lord, if it is Thy will, I will go.' Then instantly the vision vanished, and the whole chapel became filled with light so dazzling that I could faintly see the minister in the pulpit, and between him and me the glory as the light of the sun in heaven." [34]

After this vision, Evan Roberts went to Principal Evan Phillips (a mature Christian and a Moderator of the Welsh Presbyterian Church) and said, *"I keep hearing a voice telling me you must go home and speak to the young people about Christ."* He asked Principal Phillips if this was the voice of the Spirit or the devil. Principal Phillips wisely counseled him that *"The devil does not give such thoughts. It was the voice*

---

[34] Stead, *The Revival In The West*, page 45.

of the Holy Spirit."[35] So, on Monday, October 31, Evan Roberts decided to return home and conduct a week of meetings among the youth of his church.

Robert's sudden return home caught his family by surprise. His mother thought that perhaps he had been preaching somewhere on Sunday and was just calling on the family on his way back to school. But he proceeded to explain that he was home for the week, that he had experienced a very remarkable blessing, and that he had come home to lead the young people of the Moriah church in some meetings. His sister related what happened next:

"When Evan came home, Dan (his brother) was lying on the couch looking very disheartened. Evan could not understand what was wrong, and then Dan told him that he was losing his sight . . . and that a Llanelli specialist had told him that there was no hope . . . (Evan) turned towards Dan and said, 'You shall have your sight - the Lord has need of you.' Suddenly Dan regained his sight. A sort of miracle happened, and when he went to see the specialist, he marveled, unable to understand what had happened." [36]

Evan Roberts went to Pastor Daniel Jones of his own church, the Moriah Calvinistic Methodist Church in Loughor, and asked to speak to the young people. Pastor Jones was somewhat reluctant, telling Roberts that *"I might try and see*

---

[35]Ibid, page 45.

[36] Phillips, **Evan Roberts**, page 168.

what I could do, but that the ground was stony, and the task would be hard." [37] Pastor Jones told Roberts that he could speak after the Monday prayer meeting that evening to anyone who was inclined to stay. So, on Monday evening the 31st of October, 1904, Roberts spoke to 17 people who stayed after prayer meeting, telling them of his experiences and visions, and of his belief in a coming revival.

The meeting was hard. The people were unresponsive and Roberts resorted to prayer three times during his long and protracted appeal. The Welsh christians of that day had a reluctance about giving a personal testimony of assurance of salvation. But by 10 o'clock all 17 had testified of their faith in Christ, including Evan Roberts' brother, Dan, and his three sisters who publicly professed their faith for the first time. *"Young men and women who had never been known to speak openly of any experience of saving grace stood and testified fearlessly".* [38]

The first result of this personal revival was a change at home. Evan Roberts wrote to a friend, Elsie Phillips, about the events of this first week, *"Our family has had a grand change. We have had a family altar this week for the first time. This again is the work of the Spirit. And last Wednesday evening, before the meeting, while I was away from home, they held a prayer meeting at home; and father for the first time prayed in their hearing. Another proof of the grand*

---

[37] Stead, *The Revival In The West*, page 45.

[38] Matthews, *I Saw The Welsh Revival*, page 22.

work. "[39] The beginning of the greatest revival Wales had ever known had brought personal blessing to the revivalist himself and his own family.

Pastor Jones was so impressed with the power in the meeting he invited Roberts to speak again several times that week. On Tuesday, November 1, the village was agog with curious excitement. That evening he spoke at the Pisgah Chapel, which was a branch of the Moriah Chapel, closer to the Roberts home. When Evan Roberts arrived for the pre-arranged service the chapel was already besieged with curious worshipers who hardly knew what to expect. Roberts spoke on the importance of being filled with the Holy Spirit. Six people made a public confession of Christ in the meeting which lasted for three hours, from seven until ten p.m.

On Wednesday evening, November 2, he spoke at the Libanus Church in near-by Gorseinon (Pastored by Thomas Francis). After the meeting closed, Roberts led a group back to the Moriah church for an "after meeting." There Evan Roberts declared, *"I have a word for you from God."* He proceeded to give them four points, which became the basis of all his revival work:

1. You must confess any known sin to God, and put any wrong done to man right;
2. You must put away any doubtful habit;
3. You must obey the Spirit promptly;
4. You must confess your faith in Christ publicly.

---

[39] Phillips, *Evan Roberts*, page 235.

Chapter 2 - And The Fire Fell

The meeting was hard and cold, although witnesses said Roberts spoke with great power. It finished at ten o'clock.

On Thursday evening, November 3, He spoke at the Moriah Chapel upon the text, *"Ask and it shall be given you."* He exhorted the audience that *"These things must be believed, if the work is to succeed. We must believe that God is willing and able to answer our prayers."*

He also taught the assembled believers to pray a prayer that would be repeated at nearly all of Roberts meetings, *"Send the Holy Spirit to Moriah, for Jesus' sake."* By the time the meeting closed at 11 p.m. twenty people had given public testimony of Christ as Saviour.

On Friday morning, November 4, Roberts wrote to Mr. Hartley Aspden, the Editor of the **Sunday Companion** asking for a cost quotation for printing some *"Revival Picture Post-cards"*. He added, *"We are on the eve of a great and grand revival, the greatest the world has ever seen. Do not think that the writer is a madman"*.[40]

Friday evening's meeting was larger than ever, consisting of old and young from various churches and denominations. Roberts himself later described the meeting: *"The great feature of this work is that people are being awakened, and learning to obey. Those who have been with religion have had quite a new and blessed experience. They never thought what joy there was in an open confession of*

---

[40] Ibid., page 198-199.

Chapter 2 - And The Fire Fell

Christ. . . . I called these meetings for young people; but old people flock with us. . . . Last night we began at 7; finished at 10; and asked all who had confessed Christ to remain. Then the Spirit came close to us. After I had prayed, many of the people rose and went home, but about twenty remained. And we had a testimony meeting - praising the blessed Spirit for His wonderful work. The meeting finished, or rather closed, at 11:30. And we could have gone all night. Pray for our success. . . . I believe a grand blessed revival is close at hand in the near future." [41]

At the end of the week Thomas Francis, the pastor at the Libanus Church in Gorseinon, asked Roberts if he could stay on and continue the meetings for another week, rather than return to school. After an intense personal struggle he agreed, and sent a letter to his roommate, Sidney Evans, asking if Syd would join him in Gorseinon to continue the work.

On Sunday morning the Moriah Church had a previously scheduled guest speaker. But afterwards, the people asked for a special evening meeting with Roberts. One was quickly scheduled. In the meeting, which lasted for over six hours, Roberts went around the crowd of people, urging them to confess Christ. The meeting closed at eleven thirty. Roberts urged the sixty or so who had professed Christ to remain. At midnight Roberts led the congregation in a round of prayer for the Holy Spirit. Each person was to pray the same prayer, *"Send the Holy Spirit now, for Jesus Christ's*

---

[41] Ibid., page 235-236.

sake. " The second round of prayer was modified to say, *"Send the Holy Spirit **more powerfully** now, for Jesus Christ's sake.* " As the second round proceeded, two women were filled with the Holy Spirit and shouted for joy. The sixty remaining people crowded closely around Roberts. Pandemonium ruled, *"Some were shouting, 'No more Jesus, or I die!' Others cried for mercy. The noise of weeping, singing and praising, together with the sight of many who had fainted or lay prostrate on the ground in an agony of conviction was as unbelievable as it was unprecedented."* [42] The meeting finally ended in the early morning hours. It was after 3:00 a.m. when Roberts arrived home. So ended the first week of the Great Welsh Revival of 1904.

"Some Irresistible Influence"

On Monday, November 7, the normally quiet evening prayer meeting at the Moriah Church, announced for 7 p.m. was full. This was unusual for a week-night prayer meeting. News of the previous meetings had become the talk of the town, and now the growing crowds of people came with a curious anticipation, not fully knowing what to expect.

Roberts arrived at 8 p.m. and preached on the last chapter of Malachi. The meeting flowed with unusual power. Roberts urged all who had not done so to confess Christ. After a number of them had confessed, *"the place became terrible."* The congregation was moved to tears and many cried out and wept in agony. People present reported that

---

[42] Evans, *The Welsh Revival of 1904*, page 90.

they heard some powerful noise and felt the place filled with the Divine Presence. *"The people one after the other fell in agony, because of their soul's condition; and it was pitiful to see them."* Soon, Roberts asked the people to pray, *"Send the Holy Spirit now, for Jesus Christ's sake."* He prayed it first, then asked everyone present to pray it in turn. When the prayer had gone half way around the room the second time, the whole congregation gave way before *"some irresistible influence."* Many people groaned in agony, others sighed deeply, some shouted loudly, *"Pray for me,"* and a number of people wept bitterly for their sins.

It should be noted that in this meeting, for the first time in the Revival, the congregation sang what would become the most popular hymn of the day, *"**Here Is Love, Vast As The Ocean**".*

By midnight the weight of the Spirit's influence became almost unbearable and the meeting was *"boiling with fervor."* It went on until 3:00 a.m. before any attempt could be made to close it. [43]

"The Break"

But then the meetings got hard. On Tuesday night, November 8, Roberts declared *"We'll pray all night if necessary".* Despite prolonged prayers, *"heaven was as brass above them".* His mother left the meeting at 3:00 a.m. declaring, *"The people are sleeping, and it will soon be time*

---

[43] Phillips, ***Evan Roberts***, page 205-206.

for them to go to their work". The meeting broke up around 4 a.m. (Roberts later described it as *"Praying hard until four in the morning without any visible effect."*[44]).

Evan, and his brother Dan who was now assisting in the meetings, got home around daybreak. At 10:00 a.m., after only four hours of sleep, they found their mother in the downstairs parlor weeping for fear of her life, fearing that she had grieved the Holy Spirit and that her sons were more zealous for the Lord than she was. *"What weighted on my mind,"* she said, *"after leaving the chapel, was the idea that Christ stood in the Garden in His agony, and I not staying in chapel until the end of the service."*[45] They prayed and sang with her until she was comforted.

But that night "the break" had come. Revival had begun to break out elsewhere, completely independent of Roberts and his personal ministry. Pastor Thomas Francis spoke of the outburst of spiritual energy which had been felt in nearby Gorseinon that very night, *"In the prayer meeting there was grave silence, with each child present in communion with God, asking Him to send the Holy Spirit for Jesus Christ's sake. God answered their prayer and He descended on sons and daughters of all ages alike. We had*

---

[44]Ibid., page 231

[45] Ibid., page 207

never seen such weeping and singing and praying before. "[46]

Roberts was now preaching nightly, chiefly concerning obedience to the Holy Spirit. On Wednesday the 9th in Brynteg, great crowds of people from around the country side crowded into the Brynteg Congregational Chapel to hear him. Roberts stopped the Reverend Mr. Stephens from calling on anyone to open the service, and told him that his difficulty would soon be not to get people to take part in the meetings, but to stop them! The service was powerful, and the melting power of the singing was sweeping. Those present never forgot the powerful rendering of *"Here is love vast as the ocean"*. The meeting lasted till way past midnight (Roberts didn't open his Bible to read until midnight).

On Thursday, November 10, a column appeared in the local English-speaking newspaper:

A WONDERFUL PREACHER

GREAT CROWDS DRAWN TO LOUGHOR

Congregation stays till Half-past Two in the Morning.

A remarkable religious revival is now taking place in Loughor. For some days a young man named Evan Roberts, a native of Loughor, but at present a student at Newcastle-Emlyn, has been causing great surprise by his extraordinary

---

[46] *Y Diwygiad a'r Diwygwyr*, 1906, page 59, quoted by Evans, *The Welsh Revival of 1904*, page 91.

Chapter 2 - And The Fire Fell

orations at the Moriah Chapel, that place of worship having been besieged by dense crowds of people unable to obtain admission. Such excitement has prevailed that the road on which the chapel is situated has been lined with people from end to end.

Roberts, who speaks in Welsh, opens his discourse by saying that he does not know what he is going to say but that when he is in communion with the Holy Spirit, the Holy Spirit will speak, and he will simply be the medium of His wisdom. The preacher soon after launches into a fervent and at times impassioned oration. His statements have most stirring effects upon his listeners, many who have disbelieved Christianity for years again returning to the fold of their younger days. One night, so great was the enthusiasm invoked by the young revivalist that, after his sermon which lasted two hours, the vast congregation remained praying and singing until two thirty in the morning. Shopkeepers are closing up early in order to get a place in the chapel. Tin and steel workers throng the place in working clothes. The only theme of conversation among all classes and sects is "Evan Roberts." Even the taprooms of the public-houses are given over to the discussion on the origin of the powers possessed by him. Although barely in is majority, Roberts is enabled to attract the people for many miles around. He is a Methodist, but the present movement is participated in by ministers of all the Non-conformist denominations in the locality. Brynteg Chapel, Gorseinon is to be the next scene of his ministrations"[47]

Thursday evening's meeting was again held at Brynteg. Many visitors came from the surrounding district to see the revival for themselves, and to judge the "mental condition" of the Revivalist. The heavenly, spiritual influences were again intense. Roberts walked back and forth among the people, Bible in hand. At one point in the meeting someone rose and expressed the general sentiment of the people regarding Roberts himself. He said that many people thought that Roberts was becoming insane. *"But,"* he went on, *"I saw many like him in the Revival of 1859, hence do not fear anything."* [48] Roberts enjoyed a good laugh at the description.

"O Lord, Save The Reporter"

On that same Thursday a journalist came down from Cardiff, the capital of Wales, from the national daily, *The Western Mail.* He attended the Thursday evening meeting at the Brynteg Congregational Church.

According to the recorded testimony of Rhys Penry, who attended that Thursday evening meeting in Brynteg, something remarkable happened to that reporter. *"My father was at Evan Roberts' side in the meeting. At the end a reporter came up to Evan and asked, 'What can I put in the*

---

[47]*Western Mail*, Thursday, November 10, 1904, page 4.

[48] Phillips, *Evan Roberts*, page 209.

Chapter 2 - And The Fire Fell

Western Mail.' Instead of answering him, Evan prayed, 'O Lord, save the reporter' - and he was saved and went home.'![49] On Saturday, his report, which was extensive, ran two columns and featured a photograph of Evan Roberts, appeared in the newspaper as follows:

REVIVAL SCENES AT LOUGHOR

MAGNETIC PREACHING OF MR. EVAN ROBERTS

RELIGIOUS ECSTASY: ALL-NIGHT SERVICES

Our Llanelly reporter writes: The ancient township of Loughor, near Llanelly, is just now in the throes of a truly remarkable "revival," the influence of which is spreading to the surrounding districts. Meetings are being held every night attended by dense crowds, and each of them is continued well into the early hours of the next morning. The Missioner is Mr. Evan Roberts, a young man who for some years worked at the Broadoak Colliery. He has spent the whole of his life in the place, and was always known as a man with strong leanings toward religion. He is now preparing for the ministry at a preparatory school at Newcastle Emlyn. Whatever the source of his power may be, there can be no mistaking the fact that he has moved the whole community by his remarkable utterances, and scores of people who have never been known

---

[49] Jones, *Voices From The Welsh Revival*, page 29 - 30.

to attend any place of worship are now making public profession of conversion . . . .

The meeting at Brynteg Congregational Church on Thursday night was attended by those remarkable scenes which have made previous meetings memorable in the life history of so many of the inhabitants of the district. The proceedings commenced at seven o'clock, and they lasted without a break until 4:30 Friday morning. During the whole of this time the congregation were under the influence of deep religious fervor and exaltation. There were about 400 people present when I took my seat in the chapel about nine o'clock. Mr. Roberts is a young man of rather striking appearance. He is tall and distinguished looking, with an intellectual air about his clean-shaven face. His eyes are piercing in their brightness, and the pallor of his countenance seemed to suggest that these nightly vigils are telling upon him. There was, however, no suggestion of fatigue in his conduct of the meeting. There is nothing theatrical about his preaching. He does not seek to terrify his hearers, and eternal torment finds no place in his theology. Rather does he reason with the people and show them a more excellent way. I had not been many minutes in the building before I felt that this was no ordinary gathering. Instead of the set order of proceedings to which we are accustomed at the orthodox religious service, everything here was left to the spontaneous impulse of the moment. The preacher, too, did not remain in his usual seat. For the most part he walked up and down the aisles, open Bible in hand, exhorting one, encouraging another, and kneeling with a third to implore a blessing from the Throne of Grace.

Chapter 2 - And The Fire Fell

PEOPLE DROP AS IF STRUCK

A young woman rose to give out a hymn, which was sung with deep earnestness. While it was being sung several people dropped down in their seats as if they had been struck, and commenced crying for pardon. Then from another part of the chapel could be heard the resonant voice of a young man reading a portion of scripture. . . Finally, Mr. Roberts announced the holding of future meetings, and at 4:25 in the morning the gathering dispersed. But even at this hour the people did not make their way home. When I left to walk back to Llanelly I left dozens of them about the road still discussing what is now the chief subject in their lives. They had come prepared with lamps and lanterns, the lights of which in the early hours of darkness were weird and picturesque.

GENERAL REVIVAL ANTICIPATED

In the course of a conversation with our representative on Friday afternoon Mr. Roberts said that he believed we were on the eve of one of the greatest revivals that Wales had ever seen. . . . There can be no question of the reality of the visitation."[50]

On Friday, November 11, prayer meetings were held in private homes around Loughor with people praying for the

---

[50] **Western Mail**, Saturday, November 12, 1904, page 5. This article, in its essence, also appeared in the newspaper the **Llanelly Mercury**, 17 November, 1904. Your author read and compared both original articles.

salvation of friends and family members. That night some 800 people crowded the new Moriah Chapel, as it was larger than the old Moriah church, disregarding time, hunger and physical fatigue. Many ministers from the local area attended the meeting. The outstanding feature of the meeting was the "terrible bending" of a great number of people. *"Some were on their knees for a long time, unable to utter a word, owing to their soul's distress and agony. Others did their best to help, and lead them out of their pitiful state. Some fell helplessly under the powerful, divine influence, and others cried groaningly, so that one could hear them from a great distance."* [51] The service went on in this "boiling spiritual condition" until five o'clock on Saturday morning. Afterwards, a local minister declared that the community had been converted into a praying multitude.

On Saturday, November 12, every grocery store in that town was emptied *"of everything that was in an eatable state"* by people coming to the meeting. Now the entire atmosphere of the district has changed. *"Some devotional solemnity has possessed the inhabitants, and all the talk is of the Revival. Prayer meetings are held in some houses in the town all day long. The longing of the people for the salvation of their relatives and others is uncontrollable."* [52] Young people held open-air evangelistic meetings outside of public houses ("pubs") and in local gypsy camps, with many persons confessing Christ.

---

[51] Phillips, *Evan Roberts*, page 213.

[52] Ibid., page 216.

Chapter 2 - And The Fire Fell

The chapels were overcrowded hours ahead of the scheduled services. Seeing no hope of getting everyone into even the larger new Chapel, Evan Roberts asked that the old Chapel be opened as well. Saturday evening Sidney Evans (who had been greatly touched by God under the preaching of Seth Joshua two days before Evan Roberts crisis experience) preached in one chapel while Evan Roberts preached in the other, both places experiencing *"an indescribable state of spiritual commotion."*

Many people who had come to criticize and scoff were completely carried away by the now irresistible influence present in the meeting and gave themselves to Jesus. *"Among them was a Government official, who a few nights previously went to Brynteg to see Evan Roberts, the lunatic. That night, Roberts gazed at him, and his piercing eye left a deep impression on his mind. To-night he is wholly conquered".*[53]

In Saturday night's service the voice of Sam Jenkins, who would become known in the Revival as "the Welsh Sankey" (after D.L. Moody's music leader) was heard for the first time. It was past five o'clock Sunday morning before the meetings dispersed, first to their homes and then to their regular Sunday services. People who had come from a long distance had lost all consciousness of time, and felt no inclination to go home. *"Taking in this meeting and the whole of Saturday, we can say that this day liberated all the spiritual power in Loughor to its utmost extent, and it was the means of spreading the fire to the surrounding districts.*

---

[53] Ibid., page 217.

Chapter 2 - And The Fire Fell

Those who came to the meeting from different towns and neighborhoods were most of them filled with a desire to experience the same thing in their respective churches, and in a few days their desire was realized. "[54]

On Sunday morning the 13th every church in that area was again full. Eyewitness reports of that Sunday can only begin to describe the indescribable as the Spirit of God began to move and breathe new life into old congregations: *"Young men and women were so completely roused, so quickened in their spiritual experience that they could not possibly remain passive in their seats. Thrilled with an exuberance never experienced nor even dreamed of, they felt compelled to give expression to the joy that was carrying them forward triumphantly, regardless of custom or tradition. Orthodox services were out of the question. Choruses were sung. Incomparable old Welsh hymns, taught them in their tenderest years and expressing the evangelical faith of the saints of bygone days, were repeated over and over again. The words possessed a new meaning in the light of new experience. Prayers, animated by a burning passion, such as were offered, had not been heard by that generation - living, powerful, fervent intercession that brooked no refusal . . . . "*[55]

Revival In Aberdare

Early on Sunday morning, without any sleep after the

---

[54] Ibid., page 218.

[55] Matthews, *I Saw The Welsh Revival*, page 25 - 26.

Chapter 2 - And The Fire Fell

Saturday evening service which had concluded at daybreak, driven by a Loughor layman and accompanied by five young revival firebrands, Evan Roberts headed for Swansea to board a train for the Aberdare region of Wales. A Church of his own denomination, the Calvinistic Methodists, in Trecynon, a suburb of the mining town of Aberdare, had read the accounts in *The South Wales News* and *The Western Mail* of the revival taking place in Loughor. The pastor of the Aberdare church, Pastor John Morgan, had written to pastor Jones at the Moriah Chapel asking if Roberts might be available, *"We in Bryn Seion, Aberdare, have been disappointed at the last minute by the brother we expected next Sunday, November 13th, and it is a special Sunday here. Can you succeed in getting him (Evan Roberts) to come to us to the above place, Sunday?"* [56] Roberts agreed.

Roberts was accompanied by young lady converts mightily inspired by the revival and brimming over with the joy of the Lord. The sober and sedate Calvinistic congregation hardly knew what to expect. When they arrived they found their minister's place occupied by a young man, accompanied by two young revival firebrands, who exhorted all present to *"be obedient to the Holy Spirit"*. Instead of announcing the usual hymn, which all expected, one of the young women burst forth in a spiritual song, expressing her new found experience, tears streaming down her cheeks.

The congregation breathed deeply and heavily and Roberts stood absolutely silent. Soon, a strange stillness fell

---

[56] Phillips, *Evan Roberts*, page 215.

upon the church, *"like the quiet presaging an electrical storm."*[57] The storm broke in Divine fury when one of the proudest members of the congregation fell on her knees in agonizing prayer and confessed her sins. Others quickly followed. Soon, pandemonium ruled all over the chapel as men and women, young and old, knelt in the pews and aisles, claiming the blessings which now flowed from the Throne of Grace.

Burning confessions were followed by the spontaneous singing of hymns. The service continued without a break all day. By evening other churches had heard the news. A terrible crush developed as the entire neighborhood converged on the chapel. The meeting continued late into the evening.

On Tuesday, November 15th, Roberts ministered at the Ebenezer Congregational Church in Trecynon, Aberdare. The church could seat 1,000. Immense crowds poured into the town. In the evening service Roberts announced a hymn, *"Heavenly Jesus, ride victorious"*. Praise and prayer broke out spontaneously. At an intense moment in the service Roberts publicly announced that a great awakening was coming to all of Wales and that they in Aberdare were only opening the gates for it.

On Wednesday, the 16th, Evan Roberts left Aberdare for Pontycymer. But the revival in Aberdare did not stop with the departure of Roberts. Indeed, in many ways it had

---

[57] Matthews, *I Saw The Welsh Revival*, p. 29.

scarcely begun. A wonderful outpouring of the Holy Spirit occurred in Trecynon in the following days, resulting in scores of conversions, including sceptics, backsliders, and drunkards. One noted agnostic burned all of his books, and went around to neighboring places, offering Christ to sinners.[58] Area churches were completely renewed. Pastor Grawys Jones of Aberdare described what occurred when he and his fellow pastors returned to the pulpit to supervise the revival meetings after the departure of Evan Roberts:

"Some most strange joy took possession of the whole congregation. The only way I can describe it is this - as if a great shower were coming down the valley here - I have seen it often - and you can hear the noise of it in the wind, and then by and by a few big drops come, the fore-runner of the great shower. Exactly like that it came. I knew that something greater was approaching. We could hardly hold ourselves together. The praying continued, and just then, one young man who was a very splendid singer and a very fervent Christian began to sing upstairs. It took hold of the congregation, and they jumped to their feet and sang right on for about a quarter of an hour. Some were shouting for joy, and others praying. We three ministers in the pulpit were crying for joy, the tears running down our faces. We were lost to everything, and forgot all about this world, I think. The joy of it, the immense, untold joy of it was something that I never, never dreamed possible, and I doubt whether I could experience it again. It was something once for all. We never thought of time, or of drawing the meeting to a close. It never

---

[58] Phillips, *Evan Roberts*, page 256.

occurred to us at all. However, about 3:30 (a.m.) It came to a close of itself, like putting one hand in the other, and we all got up and went home. And out in the roads I could hear companies of people going down to Aberdare and singing, companies going to the east and to the north and to Cwmdar. About 4 o'clock I went home, and I could hear companies in the early morning singing away with all their might. I went to bed but could hardly sleep, and when I did I was laughing for joy in my sleep, and I got up in the morning full of joy."[59]

From this point onwards, Evan Roberts, his brother Dan and Sidney Evans traveled from church to church and town to town speaking to full crowds. The great Welsh Revival of 1904 was underway and spreading like a fire among dry tinder. It was mid-November of 1904.

From this point on until the end of December, 1904, Evan Roberts' schedule looked like a travel log for nearly every small village and town in South Wales:

November 14 & 15th, Trecynon; November 16th - 18th, Pontycymmer; November 19th, Bridgend, Pyle, Abergwynfi November 20th, Abercynon; November 21st & 22nd, Mountain Ash; November 23rd & 24th, Ynysybwl; November 25th, ill (is it any surprise?); November 26th, Cilfyngdd; November 27th & 28th, Porth; November, 29th, Treorky; December 2nd - 4th, Pentre; December 5th & 6th,

---

[59] M. Holyoak, *The Afterglow: Gleanings from the Welsh Revival* (London: Marshall Brothers, 1907), page 26, quoted by Jones, *Voices From The Welsh Revival*, page 174-175.

Caerphilly; December 7th, Senghenydd; December 8th to 10th, Ferndale; December 11th, Mardy; December 12th and 13th, Tylorstown; December 14th & 15th, Aberfan; December 16th & 17th, Hafod (Pontypridd); December 18th, Pontypridd; December 19th & 20th, Clydach Vale; December 21st, Tonypandy; December 22nd, Penygraig; December 23rd, Treherbert. [60] Roberts spent Christmas with his family in Loughor, attending services at the Moriah Chapel.

What were the "tangible results" of this fire which blazed across South Wales? According to surveys and reports by the churches in these areas, published in the *Western Mail*, from early November until the end of December 1904 (a period of roughly 60 days!), approximately 34,131 persons had made profession of faith in Christ and united with churches in membership. But even these reports were understated in that many small churches in the affected areas issued no written reports. [61]

---

[60]Stead, *Revival in the West*, page 61.

[61] Phillips, *Evan Roberts*, pages 455-456.

Chapter 3
Days Of Grace

Heavenly Jesus Ride Victorious,
Gird Thee on Thy mighty sword!
Sinful Earth can ne'er oppose Thee;
Hell itself quakes at Thy word.

Thy great name is so exalted,
Every foe shrinks back in fear.
Terror creeps through all creation,
When it knows that Thou art near.

Free my soul from sin's foul bondage;
Hasten now the glorious dawn!
Break proud Babel's gates asunder;
Let the massive bolts be drawn!

Forth, like ocean's heaving surges,
Bring in myriads ransomed slaves;
Host on host, with shouts of triumph;
Endless, countless as the waves.

William Williams
Heavenly Jesus Ride Victorious
Popular hymn during the Welsh Revival

"Like Ocean's Heaving Surges"

Revival proceeded to sweep the country, *"like ocean's heaving surges,"* with spontaneous prayer, increased crowds, conversions, confessions and quickenings. People thronged the churches day and night, far beyond the registered capacity of the buildings, without any decrease for months on end.

Dr. J. Edwin Orr states that this went on for 18 months, roughly from November of 1904 until April of 1906. Historian Brynmor P. Jones places the height of the revival in the six months from December of 1904 until May of 1905. His observations on the scope of the revival and the role of people involved are significant:

"The present age has conditioned us to find a single, charismatic personality behind each revival, but in 1904 that model would not pass the most elementary statistical test. From late December 1904 to May 1905, the period which spans the revival, a minimum of six meetings was held each day in many large industrial villages and even more in big towns, not counting overflow meetings and all-night meetings. A conservative estimate would suggest a hundred such communities in all Wales holding five hundred seiadau (meetings for sharing fellowship and experiences), prayer meetings and open-air services per day for one hundred days. It is worth recording that about one in twenty of the population yielded to Christ at this time. Evan Roberts and all his associates could not have been present or even nearby in more than 10% of these instances, with perhaps another 10% sparked off by a homecomer's testimony or by someone reciting stories of Roberts from a letter or newspaper. Yet the remaining 80% all witnessed and experienced the same spiritual phenomena. In every town rose sounds of ecstatic praise, weeping confession and earnest vows; everywhere

hardened sinners were struck down. " [62]

The normal order of church services had to be abandoned as the spirit of God took control of people, churches and meetings. *"In all Wales, songs of praise raised in ceaseless chorus from the burning hearts of countless thousands were heard in homes and churches and even in the coal mines. There are few, if any, parallels with this mighty outpouring of religious fervor, bringing a whole nation to its knees at the foot of the cross in adoration and praise. "*[63]

People lost all sense of time, physical fatigue or hunger. *"Happenings in churches everywhere made one utterly oblivious of the passage of time. No one bothered about the clock. Hours passed like minutes. The ticking of the sanctuary timepiece was drowned in an avalanche of praise . . . . When a 'man of God' receives divine unction for the delivery of his Master's message, a watch on one's wrist may be a positive nuisance. "* [64]

"Irradiated With Joy"

The Welsh were by nature sober, Bible-based believers. But Evan Roberts and his team of young people were enthusiastic and joyous. Evan Roberts could be subject

---

[62] Jones, *Voices From The Welsh Revival*, page 65-66.

[63] Matthews, *I Saw The Welsh Revival*, page 11.

[64] Ibid., p. 44.

to extreme mood swings ranging from agonizing prayer where he would weep and sweat until he almost felt he was bleeding, to ecstasy when the Holy Spirit filled his heart. He would often smile when he prayed and laugh when he preached.

One American visitor wrote, *"Evan Roberts stood in the pulpit and led the music, his face irradiated with joy, smiles and even laughter. What impressed me most was his utter naturalness, the entire absence of solemnity. He seemed to be bubbling over with sheer happiness, like a jubilant young man at a baseball game."*

The progress of the revival in any particular church did not depend upon Roberts' immediate involvement or participation. Sometimes he would attend a meeting, only to sit quietly, praying silently or singing with the congregational hymns, and then leaving without ever having said a word. Evan Roberts would not announce where he was preaching, and was known to cancel speaking engagements when he learned from the local pastor that people were coming to the meeting just to see or hear Roberts.

He shunned personal publicity and preached spontaneously and unannounced wherever the Spirit led him to show up. Within weeks of the onset of the Revival Evan Roberts had become the world's most publicized preacher, yet he repeatedly refused to give interviews to newspaper men from every part of Britain and neighboring Europe who came to see him and record the events around him. Roberts even refused to be photographed except by his own family. [65] He avoided publicity, dreaded newspaper reporters and feared the praise of the masses, solemnly warning a church on one occasion that the Holy Spirit would withdraw from the whole movement if people became the focus of attention.

"Where Is He Preaching?"

An English Baptist pastor, the Reverend H. J. Galley of Bath related to Dr. J. Edwin Orr how he journeyed by train to South Wales to meet a former classmate from Spurgeon's College.

The Welshman was full of joy. *"I have come a long way, and I would like to hear Evan Roberts preach. Where is he preaching?"* the Englishman inquired. He was surprised when his friend professed ignorance of Roberts whereabouts. *"He does not tell people where to expect him. He tells them that they need the Lord Jesus Christ, and that they will find Him in the nearest church."* Galley must have looked disappointed, for his Welsh friend added: *"Look, I can not promise that Evan Roberts will be in my church tonight, but the Spirit of God will be there in mighty power."* He then proceeded to amaze his London guest by claiming that every church in town was filled each evening until midnight, and

---

[65] Orr, *The Flaming Tongue*, page 22. Newspapermen followed him around anyway and many pictures appeared, only because they were taken without his knowledge or consent. One of the few "sitting" photographs of Evan Roberts appears on the cover of *The Institute Tie*, the forerunner of *Moody* magazine, in the March, 1905 issue.

that lesser meetings went on all day from daybreak.

"Is Jesus Here?"

In an example of Roberts self-effacing ministry, on one occasion Roberts addressed a crowded church in his deep Welsh voice with a question, *"How many of you believe the promises of God?"* A shout of agreement arose from the crowd. *"Would you agree that a promise by our Lord Jesus is especially precious?"* *"Yes!"* the congregation responded. *"Do you remember a promise of Jesus that where two or three are gathered together he is there in the midst of them?"* *"Yes!"* they responded. *"Do you believe it?"* he asked. *"Yes!"* came the response. *"I'm asking you, 'Do you believe it'?"*, he demanded. *"Yes! We believe it!"* the congregation roared back. *"Well, do we have the two or three?"* he asked. A wave of laughter rose from the crowd, as there were two or three thousand present in the church. *"Then, is Jesus here?"* he demanded. *"Yes!"* came the response. Unsatisfied Roberts asked again, *"I'm asking you, is Jesus here?"* *"Yes!"* the congregation roared back. *"Well then"* said the revivalist, *"you don't need me."* He then put on his hat and coat and went to another meeting! Did the congregation leave? No. They realized that Jesus was indeed present and the service continued on for several hours in prayer, praise and singing.[66]

---

[66] J. Edwin Orr, *"Spiritual Awakenings of the 20th Century,"* No. 2, *"The Welsh Revival"* June 19, 1973, Audio Tape Series available from Integrated Resources, the audio tape ministry of Campus Crusade for Christ International (800)729-4351.

Chapter 3 - Days Of Grace

"Can You Sing?"

The Welsh are a very musical people, and worshipful singing was a feature of the revival. As the Holy Spirit moved, it was common to find part of the congregation singing a hymn in rapturous awe, while others were on the floor crying in agony for God's mercy. An eye-witness recalled, *"Such marvelous singing, quite unrehearsed, could only be created by the Holy Spirit. No choir, no conductor, no organ - just spontaneous, unctionised soul-singing. Singing, sobbing, praying intermingled with intercession."*[67] Singing was a fruit of the revival. Many of those powerfully filled by the Holy Spirit recorded their experiences, especially of how they trembled, laughed and sang for hours afterwards.

One hymn in particular became the unofficial "theme song" of the revival, *"Dyma gariad fel y moroedd"* ("Here Is Love, Vast As The Ocean"). The words are as follows:

Here is love, vast as the ocean,
Loving-kindness as the flood,
When the Prince of Life, our ransom,
Shed for us His precious blood:
Who His love will not remember?
Who can cease to sing His praise?
He can never be forgotten
Thro' heav'n's everlasting days.

---

[67] Matthews, *I Saw The Welsh Revival*, p. 62.

Chapter 3 - Days Of Grace

On the mount of Crucifixion
Fountains opened deep and wide;
Through the floodgates of God's mercy
Flowed a vast and gracious tide;
Grace and love, like mighty rivers,
Poured incessant from above;
And heaven's peace and perfect justice
Kissed a guilty world in love. [68]

Evan Roberts himself felt singing to be of massive importance for the release of God's power. When a Londoner asked him one day if the revival could ever reach the capital, he smiled and asked, *"Can you sing?"*

London Journalist W.T. Stead made a similar observation to the **Methodist Times** on December 15, 1904, after a trip to South Wales. The interviewer asked Mr. Stead if he felt that England lay in the path of revival which was moving like a storm. *"Can our people sing? That is the question to be answered before you can decide that. Hitherto the Revival has not strayed beyond the track of the singing people. It has followed the line of song, not of preaching. It has sung its way from one end of South Wales to the other."*[69]

---

[68] William Rees, *"Gwilym Hiraethog,"* 1802-83; translated by William Edwards. Dr. William Edwards' English translation of this and other Welsh hymns were published in the **Baptist Times** in January and February of 1905.

[69] W. T. Stead, **The Revival In The West**, page 24.

Chapter 3 - Days Of Grace

Dr. Cynolwyn Pugh summed up the popular feeling regarding the role of music in the Revival:

"It is scarcely possible for us to give the present age any idea of the stirring effects of this singing and the saving influences that went with it. The explanation, it seems, is the fact that the Holy Spirit had taken hold not only of the singers but also the listeners: the atmosphere was such that the inspired words of the speakers and the words of the singers alike were winning their place in the minds and hearts of the people without too much effort."[70]

"Let Us Pray"

One of the phenomena of the Welsh Revival was hundreds of people engaging in simultaneous audible prayer (in other words, everyone prayed at once!).

Merthyn Lewis' father was a coal miner in the Rhondda Valley region of Wales. He worked the 6 a.m. to 3 p.m. shift. One day after arriving home in the afternoon he took a bath to wash off the coal dust, put on his Sunday clothes and said, *"Come mother, we're going to the church."* Off they went, children in tow. When they arrived at the church around 4 p.m. the meeting was well underway and the building was full. Around 7 p.m. Evan Roberts paid an unannounced visit. The building was so crowded that he couldn't get in. Finally the men hoisted him up on their shoulders and passed him along until he reached the pulpit.

---

[70] Quoted by Jones, *Voices From The Welsh Revival*, page 61.

Chapter 3 - Days Of Grace

When Roberts reached the pulpit he said one word in Welsh, three words in English, *"Let us pray."* That was the last thing anyone heard him say, because all two thousand people in the church began praying aloud. Each was praying his (or her) own prayer, but the result was harmony, not confusion.

Around 10 p.m. Evan Roberts put on his hat and coat and left the meeting (the family with whom he stayed said he sat up and prayed all night). At 2 a.m. Mr. Lewis turned to his wife and said, *"Come, mother, we must go home."* They arrived home around 3 a.m. Mr. Lewis slept in his clothes in the rocking chair. At 6 a.m. he changed into his work clothes. At 3 p.m. he arrived home, bathed, dressed and said, *"Come, mother, we're going to the meeting."* They returned to the church around 4 p.m. to the same meeting still going strong![71]

"Send The Holy Spirit Now..."

What was the role of the Holy Spirit in the Welsh Revival of 1904? This is a critical question, and one which many present day believers are uncomfortable about answering. Many (if not all)of the men greatly used of God in the Welsh Revival had received extra-ordinary experiences of the ministry of the Holy Spirit. Each described it differently. Some described it as a "baptism" of the Holy Spirit, others as a "filling" of the Spirit, still others as extra-ordinary divine fellowship, but all regarded it as God's enduement with

---

[71] J. Edwin Orr, *"Spiritual Awakenings of the 20th Century,"* No. 2, *"The Welsh Revival"* June 19, 1973, Audio Tape Series.

power for future ministry.

Joseph Jenkins, in whose church and under whose ministry the revival began, was wonderfully touched by God in his personal devotional life. This occurred only two or three months before God greatly touched the youth of his Christian Endeavour Movement.

"While reading Andrew Murray's **With Christ In The School Of Prayer** *he felt convicted of not having fulfilled his ministry, and a book on Moody intensified this sense of guilt. He prayed as never before, and one night in particular he lost all sense of time. Having laid hold upon God he continued to wrestle until a blessing was received which equipped him with power from on high. Getting up from his knees he became aware of a blue flame which almost enshrouded him rhythmically off and on for some time. It was an experience he never forgot and could only take as being a visible sign of the intense spiritual communion which he had enjoyed with God."* [72]

In the spring of 1904, six months or so prior to the beginning of the revival, Evan Roberts had an extra-ordinary experience of communion with God. He described it in his own words:

"One Friday night last spring, when praying by my bedside before retiring, I was taken up to a great expanse - without time and space. It was communion with God. Before this I

---

[72] Evans, *The Welsh Revival of 1904*, page 57.

had a far-off God. I was frightened that night, but never since. So great was my shivering that I rocked the bed, and my brother, being awakened, took hold of me thinking I was ill. After that experience I was awakened every night a little after one o'clock. This was most strange, for through the years I slept like a rock, and no disturbance in my room would awaken me. From that hour I was taken up into divine fellowship for about four hours. What it was I cannot tell you, except that it was divine." [73]

Roberts also described his bending at *"Blaenanerch's great meeting"* as a filling of the Holy Spirit. He acknowledged several specific effects of this filling: [74]

1. Loss of all physical weakness.
2. Physical freedom and the loss of all physical impediments.
3. Loss of all nervousness in public.
4. Physical strength in speaking, praying and singing.
5. Courage to carry out his convictions.
6. Fullness of joy.
7. Lack of anxiety regarding the future.
8. An intense desire to save souls.

Each specific effect of this filling of the Holy Spirit in Roberts' life represented an equipping or empowerment for his future ministry during the revival. Each area had been a

---

[73] Ibid., page 65-66.

[74] Phillips, **Evan Roberts**, page 126-127.

prior weakness in his life, which now became a strength for future ministry.

Later, when asked about the role of the Holy Spirit in the great revival, Roberts himself answered:

"The baptism of the Holy Spirit is the essence of revival, for revival comes from a knowledge of the Holy Spirit and the way of co-working with Him which enables Him to work in revival power. The primary condition of revival is therefore that believers should individually know the baptism of the Holy Ghost." [75]

Praying for the coming and the ministry of the Holy Spirit was at the heart of Evan Robert's ministry as a revivalist. A good example of his normal procedure occurred early in the revival at the Moriah Chapel on Sunday evening, November the sixth. The entire evening was characterized by remarkable incidents. Around midnight Roberts encouraged the congregation to begin praying for the Holy Spirit. Each person was to pray, *"Send the Holy Spirit now, for Jesus Christ's sake."* Roberts himself described what happened:

"The prayer began with me. Then it went from seat to seat - boys and girls - young men and maidens. Some asking in silence, some aloud, some coldly, some with warmth, some formally, some in tears, some with difficulty, some adding to it, boys and girls, strong voices, then tender voices. Oh, wonderful! I never thought of such an effect. I felt the place

---

[75] Whittaker, **Great Revivals**, page 108.

beginning to be filled, and before the prayer had gone half-way through the chapel, I could hear some brother weeping, sobbing, and saying, "O dear, dear. Well, well. O dear, dear." On went the prayer, the feeling becoming more intense, the place being filled more and more. I then went to see the brother, and who should it be but David Jones! "What is the matter?" said I, "Oh!" he answered, "I have had something wonderful." After this, he said that he felt his heart was too large for his bosom. I told him, "There, you have had the Holy Spirit." "I hope so," said he. The prayer had then ended its journey but not its message. "Shall we ask again for more?" "No," said David Jones. He had had as much as he could hold. But there were others, who had not had enough, and I said that brother Jones had had enough, but that we could go on to ask for more, and that Jones could ask God to with-hold, if necessary. God can give and withhold.[76]

It was under the ministry of Seth Joshua that Evan Roberts was "bent" and called as a revivalist. In late November, as the revival was underway and spreading, Seth Joshua traveled to the town of Ammanford to conduct meetings with John Pugh on behalf of the Forward Movement. The day before leaving for Ammanford, Seth Joshua wrote in his diary,

(November 18) ". . . I have wrestled for personal baptism of the Spirit and for a national revival. It has come

---

[76] Letter to Sydney Evans dated 7 November, quoted by Phillips, **Evan Roberts**, page 227-228.

and I rejoice."[77]

The personal baptism which Seth Joshua sought and received was to empower him in his revival ministry which quickly followed:

(November 19) "At 7:30 I went to meet the workers in the chapel. To my surprise the chapel was filled with people. Seeing my opportunity I commenced at once, and at the close fully twenty confessed Christ. There is a wonderful fire burning here. The ground is very prepared, thank God."[78]

(November 20) "This has been one of the most remarkable days of my life. Even in the morning a number were led to embrace the Saviour. In the afternoon the blessing fell upon scores of young people. The crush was very great to get into the chapel. At 7 o'clock a surging mass filled the Christian Temple, with crowds unable to gain entrance. The Holy Spirit was indeed among the people. Numbers confessed Jesus, but it is impossible to count."[79]

During the Welsh Revival of 1904 the ministry of the Holy Spirit, whether described as a "baptism" or as a "filling" was clearly evident among the revivalists, the evangelists and the people.

---

[77]Evans, *The Welsh Revival of 1904*, page 104.

[78] Ibid., page 104.

[79] Ibid., page 104-105.

Chapter 3 - Days Of Grace

Revival & Politics

A political rally arranged at Pwllheli for the Member of Parliament (later Prime Minister) David Lloyd-George transformed itself into a revival meeting. A local minister offered a devotion, the audience sang a hymn with great fervor, and a blind man led in prayer. The two notable political speakers were scarcely noticed at all.

Later Lloyd-George compared the revival to an earthquake and a tornado in its far-reaching social impact. At a public gathering in Glasgow he spoke of a town in his constituency (legislative district) where the total revenue from the sale of alcohol in the local pub (short for "public house") on a Saturday night had been only 9 cents (4 ½ pence).

The Singing Constable

In the township of Holyhead on the island of Anglesey off the northwest coast of Wales a constable was standing guard duty outside of the local court room. Suddenly he heard an outburst of singing come from inside the court. Since this was quite unusual he rushed inside to determine what had happened.

It seems that the accused prisoner had come under a deep conviction of sin and had admitted that he was a sinner. The judge gavelled the proceedings to a close and turning to the accused he said, *"As a Christian man I want to point you to Christ as Savior."* When the man professed Christ as his Savior the members of jury were overwhelmed and broke out in a glorious Welsh hymn. This was the point at which the confused constable entered the courtroom. He stayed and added his bass voice to the impromptu choir, and a praise and prayer service went on for another hour.[80]

Lack Of Human Control

Visitors flocked to Wales from every English speaking country only to be surprised at the total lack of human effort behind the revival.

Dr. F.B. Meyer, of the Keswick convention fame, visited many localities of the Revival. He commented that no money was spent on advertising the Revival meetings and that there was no need for posters. There were no handbills distributed, no hired halls and no paid staff. The Revival advertised and financed itself.

An American observer noted that the Welsh Revival was *"on the whole a movement among the people. The meetings have consisted almost entirely by prayer and praise and have been under the direct control of the Spirit of God. There is in this a very profound lesson. The average church regards revival as impossible without an evangelist. As a matter of fact, there can be one wherever there are united Christian people who are ready for it. God sends the power*

---

[80] J. Edwin Orr,*"Spiritual Awakenings of the 20th Century,"* No. 2, *"The Welsh Revival"* June 19, 1973, Audio Tape Series.

Chapter 3 - Days Of Grace

in every case, just as He has in Wales. "[81]

W.T. Stead, a London journalist, attended a church meeting in Maerdy in the Rhondda Valley region where Evan Roberts came to speak. He, too, observed the total lack of human control over the meetings: *"The most extra-ordinary thing about the meetings which I attended was the extent to which they were absolutely without any human direction or leadership. 'We must obey the Spirit' is the watchword of Evan Roberts, and he is as obedient as the humblest of his followers. The meetings open - after any amount of preliminary singing, while the congregation is assembling - by the reading of a chapter or a Psalm. Then it is go-as-you-please for two hours or more. And the amazing thing is that it does go and does not get entangled in what might seem to be inevitable confusion. Three-fourths of the meeting consists of singing. No one uses a hymn-book. No one gives out a hymn. The last person to control the meeting in any way is Mr. Evan Roberts. People pray and sing, give testimony; exhort as the Spirit moves them. As a study of the psychology of crowds, I have seen nothing like it. You feel that the thousand or fifteen hundred persons before you have become merged into one myriad-headed, but single souled personality. "*[82]

---

[81] **Baptist Commonwealth**, January 26, 1905.

[82] Stead, **The Revival In The West**, page 38 - 39.

Chapter 3 - Days Of Grace

Spiritual Gifts

The great Welsh Revival of 1904 has been described as the first major revival to emphasize the spiritual gifts. Whether or not this generalization is accurate is open to debate. But there is no question that the exercise of spiritual gifts was prevalent during the revival.

Perhaps there is no better example of the exercise of spiritual gifts during the revival than the ministry of Evan Roberts himself. Roberts appears to have exercised the charismatic gift of discernment (often referred to today as a "word of knowledge"). According to W. T. Stead, who observed and interviewed Roberts extensively, *"The truth about Evan Roberts is that he is very psychic, with clairvoyance well developed and a strong visualizing gift. One peculiarity about him is that he has not yet found any watch that will keep time when it is carried in his pocket."* [83]

At the Tuesday evening meeting at the Ebenezer Congregational Church in Aberdare (on November 15th), Roberts was ministering from the pulpit. Suddenly he addressed the congregation, *"Will someone go outside? To the left of the church you will find a woman in spiritual distress. Will you help her to find the Saviour?"* Profound silence struck the congregation, and the woman was found outside the building just as Roberts had said. Later, during the same meeting, Roberts announced, *"There is a young man in soul-distress at the far end of the gallery. He is anxious for*

---

[83] Ibid., page 54.

salvation. Will someone please help him?" The young man was indeed found and helped.[84]

On another occasion, when ministering to a crowd of over 6,000 in Liverpool, Roberts stopped the singing and asked for prayer. Suddenly he stopped the service and declared in Welsh and English that , *"there is one English friend in this meeting who tries to hypnotize me this very moment. Will you leave the building at once or ask the Lord to forgive you? God will not be mocked We don't come here to play. We come here to worship the Lord . . ."* The incident caused quite a stir in the local press, with accusations that Roberts was mentally unstable. But Roberts was later vindicated when a hypnotist appearing at the local Lyric Theatre publicly acknowledged that he had indeed been present at the meeting.[85]

Manifestations

The Welsh Revival saw strong manifestations of the out-pouring of the Holy Spirit upon the Church. The powerful work of the Spirit was evident to observers in meetings. London Journalist W. T. Stead noted that *"You can watch what they call the influence of the power of the Spirit playing over the crowded congregation as an eddying wind plays over*

---

[84]Matthews, *I Saw The Welsh Revival*, p. 38-39.

[85] Evans, *The Welsh Revival of 1904*, page 140.

the surface of a pond."[86]

Daniel Williams recorded that *"The manifestation of the power was beyond human management. Men and women were mowed down by the axe of God like a forest. The glory was resting for over two years in some localities. Ministers could not minister, like Moses, when the cloud of glory came down on the Tabernacle. The weeping for mercy, the holy laughter, ecstasy of joy, the fire descending, burning its way to the hearts of men and women with sanctity and glory, were manifestations still cherished and longed for in greater power."*[87]

The Revival unleashed new and powerful forces in the churches and chapels of Wales. Thomas Williams of Parc, Trecynon, observed the new and strange events occurring in the churches there during Evan Roberts visit in November of 1904:

"The divine assaults of the Eternal Spirit were seen striking down men like corpses all over the floor . . . The unanimous testimony of those who experienced them is that

---

[86] Stead,, *The Revival in the West*, page 39.

[87] Evans, *The Welsh Revival of 1904*, page 194. Although there were sporadic outbursts of tongues, and other charismatic gifts during the revival, Evan Roberts discouraged the exercise of the gift of tongues, *"until the spiritual section of the Church of Christ are more acquainted with the counterfeiting methods of the spirit of evil, and the laws which give them power of working, any testimony to such experiences as true, cannot be safely relied upon."*

they were pierced as by a sword or an arrow, or struck as though by a shot from a cannon . . . One knows of some meetings where there were reasonable grounds for believing that something like an impairment of the senses had taken place in them; and not a few were frightened at the sights they saw. . .". [88]

Evan Roberts was acutely aware of the potential danger of manipulating a service either to foster spiritual excitement or to promote or emphasize spiritual manifestations. He observed that *"When there comes a pause in the services, then is there a danger of someone swinging the pendulum instead of raising the weights."* [89]

Roberts himself experienced a variety of manifestations, while at the same time exhorting individuals to maintain decency and order. W. T. Stead observed Roberts in one particular meeting and noted,

"He dwells sometimes on the sufferings of Christ until he falls prone, sobs choking his utterance. While absolutely tolerant of all manifestations of the Spirit, he is stern to check disorder. At Ferndale, where some persons had been disturbing the meeting by exuberant and unseemly noises, he said: 'He who would walk with God must come to His house

---

[88] T. Williams, *Adgofion am Ddiwygiad 1904-05 yn Nhrecynon* (Dolgellau: E. W. Evans, 1913), pp. 55-56, quoted by Jones, *Voices From The Welsh Revival*, page 159.

[89] Phillips, *Evan Roberts*, page 485.

in a spirit of prayer, of humility, or awe. Joy is permissible in the house, but it must be sanctified joy. For think of the majesty of the Divine Person . . . . we are taught to entreat for the descent of the Spirit, but beware lest the entreaty becomes a rude, imperious command. If we truly walk with God, there can be no disorder, no indecency. ' "[90]

"Conviction Is Not Conversion"

The Welsh Revival particularly saw extra-ordinary scenes of individuals overwhelmed by a deep conviction of sin. Dr. G. Campbell Morgan reported that, *"The movement is characterized by the most remarkable confessions of sin, confessions that must be costly. I heard some of them, more rising who have been members of the church and officers of the church, confessing hidden sin in their hearts, impurity committed and condoned, and seeking prayer for its putting away. "*[91]

Such situations held the potential for emotional excess being mistaken for genuine spiritual conversions. But Seth Joshua, E. Keri Evans and other mature and prominent evangelists were used by God to exercise a steadying influence through their Bible teaching. Solid Bible teaching became the moderating influence to channel the powerful

---

[90] Stead, *The Revival In The West*, page 50.

[91] G. Campbell Morgan, Sermon In Westminster Chapel, London, December 25, 1904, quoted by Orr, *The Flaming Tongue*, page 20.

emotions generated by the revival. Commenting upon this E. Keri Evans recalled: *"I was invited to meetings up and down the land and proclaimed chiefly, 'Conviction is not conversion'* . . . *adding, 'nor is awakening, repentance'* . . . *there were many* . . . *who had been on the crest of a wave of jubilation for well-nigh a whole year, and when the jubilation subsided sought to regain it by artificial means, not realizing that the Holy Spirit works through the imagination and emotion to the conscience to produce repentance, and through the conscience to the will in order to lead to conversion."* [92]

"I Want To Ask A Question!"

The power of the Revival for evangelism took many forms, but was unmistakable. An unusual form of evangelism occurred at that Wednesday meeting at the Ebenezer Congregational Church in Aberdare. Evan Roberts was standing in the pulpit of the crowded church and had just finished reading from 1 Corinthians 13 when a booming voice was heard coming from the gallery. *"I want to ask a question!"* it declared for all to hear. Members moaned and hearts sank as the congregation recognized the speaker as a prominent local agnostic. Roberts stood unruffled as the congregation began singing a popular revival melody. Again the voice boomed above the song, *"If you do not answer me, I will come to the pulpit to ask my question."* As no one responded to his outburst, he proceeded to make good his threat. He moved toward the gallery stairs through the dense

---

[92] Evans, *The Welsh Revival of 1904*, page 137.

crowd with the intent of reaching the Deacon's pew, if not the pulpit itself.

Mid-way down the stairs something happened. In a word, the Holy Spirit met the agnostic and the gallery stairs were transformed into the Damascus road. He collapsed, crying out for mercy and pardon. When those around him realized what had happened a shout went up, *"He has been saved! He has been saved!"* Pandemonium ruled as restraint yielded to joy, tears, laughter, songs and sobs. And sinners throughout the building began to cry out, *"What must I do to be saved?!"* as the river of God's Spirit flowed through the Ebenezer Congregational Church of Aberdare on that November evening of 1904.[93]

Resistance

The Welsh Calvinistic Methodist Church (later known as the Presbyterian Church in Wales) fully supported the 1904-5 revival, including the work of Evan Roberts (in spite of the fact that he never took denominational ordination, and never finished his studies at Newcastle Emlyn College), as well as the work of other revival leaders and evangelists. The Congregationalists and the Wesleyan Methodists also supported the revival, while the Quakers declared, *"What we have seen in Wales is Quakerism rebaptized! . . . . The iron in*

---

[93] Matthews, *I Saw The Welsh Revival*, p. 36-37. David Matthews was personally present at this meeting and relates this story as an eyewitness.

our Welsh valleys is hot. Let us strike before it cools." [94]

The Anglican Bishop of Dorking was so intrigued by reports of the revival that he spent three days traveling *incognito* through the valleys and mining villages of Wales, visiting four chapels of different affiliations, finding them filled every night with people engaged in prayer, praise, testimony and exhortation.

On another separate occasion some persons were giving unbridled rein to their spiritual impulses, to the annoyance of the whole congregation. When the church leadership asked them to restrain their exuberance the Tory daily newspaper for South Wales (the official organ of the Church of England) rebuked the leadership for attempting to quench the Spirit!

The Archbishop of Canterbury himself asked for prayer that an awakening would move all of Great Britain. The Bishop of Durham described the Revival as a movement of God, and noted that *"it was no fanaticism or fancy that caused white gloves to be presented to County Court judges"*[95]

Acceptance of and participation in the Revival was general and widespread, but it was not universal. And as the Revival spread, so did resistance. A resident of Llangollen

---

[94] Orr, *The Flaming Tongue*, page 19.

[95] *The Christian*, February 9, 1905, page 24.

wrote to the local newspaper complaining that he had been "forced" to dismiss one of his domestic servants who was spending (in his opinion) too much time at the meetings and was *"invariably coming home an hour or so late. My friends tell me they have the same thing to face . . ."* Others complained of the emotional excesses, still others about the manifestations. Rationalists and agnostics openly ridiculed the Revival.

Several university "dons" (tenured professors) and their student followers regarded the emotionalism and manifestations as resembling "mental illness," "mass-hysteria," or the spreading of an "epidemic disease." The British medical journal *"The Lancet"* even joined in criticizing the Revival, with articles citing stories which suggested that there was a link between revivalism and lunacy!

Evan Roberts soon became a lightening rod for criticisms regarding the revival. On 31 January, 1905 a letter appeared in the *Western Mail*, written by Peter Price, the minister at the Dowlais Congregational Church. The letter was a bitter attack upon Evan Roberts. In essence, Price (who made certain that the reader knew he was an honors graduate of Queens College, Cambridge) claimed that there were actually two revivals in Wales. The first, which he labeled as the true revival, was the one which his own church had been experiencing for over a year, resulting in many converts. The second was the "mock revival", consisting of "false fire" and "vain trumpery," and which was led by Evan Roberts.

The letter sparked a hornet's nest of controversy. The vast majority of the Welsh people supported Roberts and the Revival, but critics used the controversy as a rallying point. When asked about it, Evan Roberts simply said, *"Let him alone. I have my work to do."* [96] Roberts never offered any other response, although the attack hurt him deeply.

In mid-February a letter appeared from Pastor J.Towyn Jones who wisely observed that the root of the problem might, in part, be the press coverage of the Revival. He pointed out that press sought to emphasize and exaggerate Evan Roberts' desire to make people look only to the Holy Spirit for guidance in the Revival and not to men. In addition, he observed that the press was attempting to credit one man (i.e., Evan Roberts) with the pentecostal fire of revival and to make that one man indispensable.[97]

A column by a sympathetic pastor in the *Llanelly Mercury* newspaper in March summed up the majority of complaints regarding the revival:

"Some object to the beloved young man, whom the Lord has chosen to spread the heavenly fire and light abroad . . . Some object to women taking part in public prayer, exhortation, testifying, or reading of the Word . . . Some persons object to so much singing in the daily meetings . . . Some object to the

---

[96] *Christian Herald*, London, February 16, 1905, quoted by Orr, *The Flaming Tongue*, page 23.

[97] Jones, *Voices From The Welsh Revival*, page 271.

length of meetings . . . Some object to the visions seen . . .
Some ridicule the idea that Mr. Evan Roberts was not allowed
to go as he wished, and intended to go to Cardiff, as if Paul,
who wished to go to Asia and Bithynia, had not been
forbidden to go there . . . Some object to the Lord's
messenger calling attention to the icy souls, whom his
anointed eyes perceive in the congregation, who, as ice,
create a unfavourable atmosphere, as if no Satan was to be
rebuked, and as if the revivalist had no message to dark
minds; stony, starchy hearts, and sleepy consciences." [98]

By The Brook Cherith

In March of 1905 reports began to surface of Roberts'
failing health. The strain of working eighteen and twenty hour
days, constant travel, irregular meals, and the personal attacks
of the Revival's critics were beginning to take their toll. He
was found physically and mentally fit by four doctors who
examined him at the request of friends. The four physicians
signed and issued a *"Certificate of Physical and Mental*
Health," causing many observers to chuckle that Roberts was
the only evangelist on record with a certificate of sanity! But
a period of rest was advised.

Roberts continued working throughout 1905 and into
1906. But in April of 1906, suffering from "nervous
prostration," he retired to private life "by the brook Cherith"
in the home of the Penn-Lewis family of Leicester. Roberts

---

[98] *Llanelly Mercury*, 16 March, 1905, quoted by Jones, *Voices*
From The Welsh Revival, page 259.

never again entered into public Christian ministry, devoting himself instead to prayer and intercession for his beloved Wales.

To the consternation of its critics, the Revival continued without Evan Roberts. Other capable and anointed men, in whom the newspaper press were less interested, answered the growing demand for evangelists, pastors and teachers. Such outstanding evangelists as Seth Joshua, E. Keri Evans, R.B.Jones, Joseph Jenkins, W.W. Lewis, and many others filled the gap, working faithfully for long hours.

The American Evangelist Gipsy Smith conducted a series of evangelistic meetings in the Glamorgan Valley Region where he experienced an unusual measure of blessing and an unusual manifestation of power. [99] Seth Joshua, an official evangelist of the Calvinistic Methodist Church, conducted evangelistic revival meetings throughout South Wales. On one occasion he experienced having as many as twelve hundred men on their knees in simultaneous audible prayer.[100]

_____

[99] *The Christian*, January 26, 1905.

[100] *The Advance*, February 16, 1905.

Chapter 4
Afterglow

"As spring-time precedes summer, and seed-time harvest, so every great onward step in the social and political progress of Great Britain has ever been preceded by a national Revival of Religion. The sequence is as unmistakable as it is inevitable . . . . Hence it is not necessary to be Evangelical, Christian, or even religious, to regard with keen interest every stirring of popular enthusiasm that takes the familiar form of a Revival. Men may despise it, hate it, or fear it, but there is no mistaking its significance. It is the precursor of progress, the herald of advance. It may be as evanescent as the blossom of the orchard, but without it there would be no fruit."[101]

The Ethical Result

"The supreme test of a Revival," said the Reverend F. B. Meyers of Keswick Convention fame, *"is the ethical result."* By this test alone, the Welsh Revival of 1904-5 was genuine and lasting.

The impact of the Welsh Revival upon the nation was as profound as it was varied. Sales of Bibles soared to the point that stocks of Welsh and English Bibles were sold out. Prayer meetings sprang up in coal mines, in trains, on trams and in business establishments. Long-standing and bitter labor disputes were suddenly resolved. In several places judges (or "magistrates") were presented with white gloves, signifying

---

[101] Stead, ***The Revival In The West***, page 33.

that there were no cases to try.

A local minister in Bethesda declared, *"The policemen tell me that the public houses are nearly empty, the streets are quiet, and swearing is rarely heard. Things are easy for the policemen here now - I hope they have a glorious holiday, and the district is quite prepared to support them henceforth - for doing nothing!"*.[102]

In one jurisdiction the town council held an emergency meeting to discuss what to do with the police, now that they were unemployed. They interviewed a police sergeant to learn what the police were now doing. The sergeant explained that before the revival the police had two main jobs; preventing or investigating crime and crowd control. Now, he explained, because of the revival there was no crime, so the police were simply going with the crowds. *"What does that mean?"* inquired one confused councilman, *"How does that affect you?"*. The Sergeant explained that the crowds were now in the churches. So the 17 men in his precinct had formed three men's singing quartets. Now, whenever a church needed a quartet, they simply called the police station.

In the Welsh capital of Cardiff the police reported a 60% decrease in drunkenness. In Glamorgan, convictions for drunkenness fell from 10,528 in 1903 to 5,490 in 1906. In Westminster Abbey, Archdeacon Wilberforce declared that *"two months of the revival had done more to sober the*

---

[102] Evans, *The Welsh Revival of 1904*, page 110.

country than the temperance laws in two years". The new wave of sobriety which swept over Wales caused severe financial losses as many taverns were forced to close for lack of business. W.T. Stead observed,

"There is less drinking, less idleness, less gambling. Men record with almost incredulous amazement how one football (i.e., rugby) player after another has foresworn cards and drink and the gladiatorial games, and is living a sober and godly life, putting his energy into the Revival . . . . the Tory daily paper of South Wales has devoted its columns day after day to reporting and defending the movement which declares war to the death against both gambling and drink." [103]

The revival affected life in the workplace, especially in the coal mines of Wales. In his revival travels Evan Roberts would often rise early (if he ever went to bed!) and wait at the pit heads of the local coal mine at 5:00 a.m. to meet the miners as they came off of the late shift, inviting them to the meetings for that day. Many would respond and attend. *"Employers tell me that the quality of the work the miners are putting in has improved. Waste is less, men go to their daily toil with a new spirit of gladness in their labour. In the long dim galleries of the mine, where once the hauliers swore at their ponies in Welshified English terms of blasphemy, there is now but to be heard the haunting melody of the Revival music. The pit ponies, like the American mules, having been driven by oaths and curses since they first bore the yoke, are being re-trained to do their work without the*

---

[103] Stead, *The Revival In The West*, page 36.

incentive of profanity. " [104]

Cursing and profanity were so reduced among the formerly profane miners in the coal mines that it nearly caused coal production to come to a complete halt. It seems that so many miners had given up profanity and cursing that the pit ponies which pulled the coal cars in the mine tunnels could no longer understand the commands being given to them. Work slowed down until the bewildered creatures could learn the new heavenly language.

Repentance was evidenced by practical deeds and changed lives. Longstanding debts were repaid, stolen goods were returned, and numerous cases of restitution for past sins and grievances were recorded (In the village of Maesteg a businessman reported receiving a live pig in payment of a debt which had been outstanding since 1898). *"Not merely are all the grosser vices reduced to vanishing point, but the subtler sins of unforgiving rancour, non-payments of debts, dishonest work are abated."* In many jurisdictions the moral climate was so affected by the revival that the number of illegitimate births fell by 44% in the year following the outbreak of the revival.

In Swansea, the Poor Law Guardians (who administered relief to the poor) commented on an unusual occurrence; working people were taking their aged parents

---

[104] Ibid., page 35-36.

home from the workhouse to which they had been sent. [105]

In a word, the Revival united denominations, filled the churches every night, renewed family ties, changed life in the mines and factories, crowded the streets with huge processions, reduced social vices and diminished overall crime. In the words of one observer:

"Who can give an account of the lasting blessings of the 1904-05 Revival? Is it possible to tabulate a sum total of family bliss, peace of conscience, brotherly love, and holy conversation? What of the debts that were paid, and the enemies reconciled to one another? What of the drunkards who became sober, and the prodigals who were restored? Is there a balance that can weigh the burdens of sins which was thrown at the foot of the Cross?" [106]

D.E. Richards of the Baptist Union of Wales declared, *"The Moderator of the Union, the professors of our colleges, the pastors of our churches and our students are surcharged with Divine fire; the Holy Spirit seems to have possessed our pulpit completely; the Church has wakened and has put on the beautiful garments of her glory. The people repent and the thousands are baptized in the name of Jesus for forgiveness*

---

[105] Orr, *The Flaming Tongue*, page 18.

[106] Gomer M. Roberts and Sidney Evans, *Cyfrol Gofa Diwygiad 1904-5*, page 73, quoted by Orr, *The Flaming Tongue*, page 28.

of sins and the gift of the Holy Spirit. "[107]

A Steady Glow

As the Revival proceeded, things that had been "extra-ordinary" in normal times became so commonplace that they were no longer considered "newsworthy". As a result the steady growth of evangelism and conversions went unreported, except in denominational publications. By late 1906 in Wales there was talk that the fires of revival had died out. But Seth Joshua observed that *"there was no great blaze of revival enthusiasm now in Wales, just a steady glow in many places north and south."* [108]

Lasting Results

The question has been asked from time to time, usually by its critics, why the Welsh Revival didn't last. The truth is that it did last. The most intense phase of the revival was the first six months, during which 100,000 persons were added to the churches. The revival itself continued for eighteen months to two years. Even critics of the revival, such as J.V. Morgan, a friend of Peter Price (the revival's chief antagonist), admitted that eighty percent of the converts remained in the churches after five years.

---

[107] *Baptist Commonwealth*, September 7, 1905, quoted by Orr, *The Flaming Tongue*, page 19.

[108] Seth Joshua, *Missionary Review*, 1906, page 82, quoted in Orr, *The Flaming Tongue*, page 27.

Chapter 4 Afterglow

The official reports of the Churches in Wales proclaimed the lasting results of the awakening. Official reports after 2 months showed gains of 34,131 members in South Wales alone. Throughout Wales there were 70,000 converts in 2 months, 85,000 converts in 3 months, and 100,000 converts in 6 months. It is estimated that during the 18 months of the Revival itself, one in twenty persons in Wales professed faith and joined the church (or 5% of the total population of the nation).[109]

From 1903 until 1907 the five largest Church bodies in Great Britain, including Wales, England and Scotland (the Church of England, Church of Scotland & other Presbyterians, Methodists, Congregationalists, and Baptists) officially reported increased memberships of 283,799 or a percentage increase of 5.4%.

These figures, either in Great Britain as a whole or in Wales alone, do not account for the number of members who left due to immigration or falling away, nor do they reflect the number of church members who were themselves either converted or renewed by the revival.

The Fading Fires of Revival In Wales

Many misconceptions regarding the Welsh Revival

---

[109] Jones, *Voices From The Welsh Revival*, page 65. To put such a number in perspective, if 5% of the U.S. population of 1996 (264,589,473 persons) were to profess faith in Christ, this would represent 13,229,473 conversions!

have taken root over the years. On one of my research trips through England a Church of England Associate Pastor asked me why the Welsh Revival didn't last and why it burned out so quickly. The reality is that "lasted" for roughly two years in Wales, spread to nearly every country and continent, and lit worldwide fires of revival which burned until the out-break of World War I.

But like every revival since the day of Pentecost, the spreading fires of the Welsh Revival eventually died out, leaving behind changed lives, changed churches, a changed nation, and even a changed world. The legacy of renewal and revival in any generation is not the flame and the fire, but the tangible effects of transformation in lives, churches and nations.

There were factors which contributed to the fading of the fires of the Revival. Not the least of these factors was the resistance to the revival, born during the heat of the Revival itself. Even some churches that had experienced the Revival began to resist and reject those individuals who had experienced revival. There was a desire among the leadership of many churches to seek to return to the "normalcy" of church life prior to the outbreak of the Revival.

According to Nantlais Williams, *"Words often heard from the mouths of some during the first years of the Revival were, 'Oh, the Revival has ended now, everything has gone back to normal here.' For such people the Revival was nothing more than a sad misadventure which disturbed the peaceful quietude of church and country, and because they thought there was no good in it, or rather, they did not want to see any good in it, they rejoiced at the slightest sign that it was disappearing.*" [110]

Reports surfaced how deacons in some churches had begun prohibiting women from participating in services as they had during the revival. The processions of children and the ministries of young gospel singers were soon stopped. Conflicts soon arose in some churches between the *"children of the Revival,"* as they came to be known, and those in the churches who wanted to return to life as it had been. As a result, some left the "established" churches to join the "mission halls and the pentecostals".

Finally, while "falling away" (however defined) was minimal among those revived, converted or influenced by the revival, within a decade their ranks were decimated by the blood-letting unleashed by World War I, as the choicest men of that generation fell in the trenches of France and filled Flanders Fields with their honored dead.

---

[110] **Yr Efengylydd**, October 1915, page 147, quoted by Jones in *Voices From the Welsh Revival*, page 272.

Chapter 4 Afterglow

Chapter 5
Revival In America

As news of the Welsh Revival reached the United States spontaneous meetings for prayer began to break out in anticipation of what was regarded as the coming blessing. The Baptists in one of their official journals declared, *"Let us cease talking about revivalism, and get to our knees and pray for a revival."* [111]

The Southern Baptists declared in one of their state publications:

"Will the revival be repeated in this country? To answer this question, we are doing as usual the inconsistent thing. We read that the Welsh Revival grew out of prayer and has no machinery, and then we set to work to get all our machinery in motion." [112]

In New York city, the pastors of all of the protestant churches in the City met in the Marble Collegiate Church to pray for a revival in the United States. In Chicago there was an area-wide meeting in the Loop area attended by Methodist Bishop W. F McDowell and other prominent church leaders to pray for revival. The same types of spontaneous meetings

---

[111] *The Examiner*, February 2, 1905, quoted by Orr, *The Flaming Tongue*, p. 68. See also J. Edwin Orr, *"Spiritual Awakenings of the 20th Century,"* No. 3, *"Revival in America and The Home Countries"* June 20, 1973, Audio Tape Series.

[112] *Western Recorder*, Louisville, May 4, 1905, quoted by Orr, *The Flaming Tongue*, p. 68.

of pastors from all denominations, praying for the coming revival, were held in other major cities around the United States.

The first reported outbreak of revival came in December of 1904, in Wilkes-Barre, Pennsylvania. There was a significant Welsh population there due to the local coal mines. A Baptist pastor, J.D. Roberts, received word of the Revival directly from Wales. Revival broke out in his church with 123 converts in the first month. Soon, revival broke out in Scranton, Pittsburgh and New Castle. The leading Baptist newspaper, the *Baptist Commonwealth*, devoted an entire issue to revival throughout country. By spring, 1905, the Methodists in Philadelphia reported they had 6,101 new converts on probationary membership.

As 1905 unfolded, various denominational publications were filled with articles describing the unprecedented events in Wales. By Spring of 1905 the effects of the Welsh Revival were apparent and spreading throughout the United States. The spreading revival shook every mainline denomination. To take only one denominational example, the Presbyterian Church in the United States (the "PC-USA") recorded widespread revival throughout its Presbyteries, coinciding with a previously planned evangelistic program. Their timing could not have been better!

In a humorous side-note, one Presbyterian observed, *"Theoretically, we are opposed to revivals and in favor of an even and uninterrupted growth of the Churches, but unfortunately, the facts are against us."* The facts were indeed against them. The reality was that roughly one-half of the membership of the Presbyterian Church, and an equal proportion of their ministers, had "decided" during some revival. [113]

In May of 1901 the General Assembly of the Presbyterian Church had formed an Evangelistic Commission with Dr. J. Wilbur Chapman as its recognized leader. By 1902, there were 56 Presbyterian evangelists roaming the United States. In 1903, twelve hundred Presbyterian pastors united in a concert of prayer for revival. Special evangelistic services were held in 1285 Presbyterian churches, and some 1580 ministers reported decisions in excess of usual. The Baptists and Methodists even praised their Presbyterian brothers for their work. [114]

According to the 1905 minutes of the General Assembly, *"The fact that in the judgment of many we have entered upon a great world-wide awakening makes it imperative that a Committee should be appointed. (Editor's Note:* In the Presbyterian Church, even a world-wide movement of the Spirit of God must be done decently and in order, so appoint a committee!) *The great revival in England, the unprecedented revival in Wales, the awakened hopes on the part of Christians everywhere, and the remarkable*

---

[113] *Presbyterian Journal*, Philadelphia, cited in *Western Christian Advocate*, Indiana, September 19, 1900, quoted by Orr, *The Flaming Tongue*, p. 67.

[114] Orr, *The Flaming Tongue*, p. 67.

awakenings in our own country, all indicate that the best work in the interest of evangelism may yet be done". [115]

California - In Oakland the Presbyterian Church experienced extra-ordinary blessing in their organized evangelistic campaign. According to Reverend E.E. Baker, *"Thirty three churches of different denominations cooperated. Large meetings for men only, a day of prayer with closed stores, a mid-night service as well as the regular evening services which were thronged, show that our city is concerned about higher things, and that our citizens respond to the claims of religion. This simultaneous campaign, which is swaying the country from Atlanta to the sea, makes possible a larger evangelistic effort than we have yet known. We have had substantial additions already and many more will follow. The 600 received since the close of the meetings are only a beginning of the good done. Our churches have been revived. Religion has been brought to the front. Evangelism has been rehabilitated where it had been wounded in the house of its friends. The Bible is being studied as never before."* [116]

Colorado - In Denver the Mayor declared Friday, January 20, 1905 as a day of prayer. At 10:00 a.m. all churches in the city were full. At 11:30 nearly every business

---

[115] ***Minutes of the General Assembly of the Presbyterian Church in the United States***, New Series, Vol. V, No. 2, 1905, Proceedings of the 117th General Assembly, 1905, Report by the Special Committee on Evangelistic Work, page 34.

[116] Ibid., page 31.

establishment in Denver was closed. Four theaters were crowded for prayer with people who couldn't get into the churches. The Colorado Legislature voted to postpone business in order to attend the prayer meetings, and every school in Denver was closed.

The Reverend Robert F. Coyle reported to the Presbyterian General Assembly that *"The United Evangelistic Campaign in Denver made a profound impression on the city. Churches were thronged. On one day all business ceased. His Honor the Mayor and His Excellency the Governor sat with us on the platform during the special services on the day of prayer. At our midnight meeting thousands paraded the streets, and as a result of this one service scores came to Christ. My own church received one hundred and sixty at its first communion. Several thousand have already joined the Church. More are coming."* [117] The effects of this outpouring of prayer and revival power were felt for almost a year.

Connecticut- At Yale University, in New Haven, the revival deeply touched the student body. In 1905 a young transfer and scholarship student named Kenneth Scott Latourette (later a famous church historian) was the Secretary of the campus prayer and bible study groups. He stated that in 1905, one quarter (25%) of the student body was enrolled in prayer and bible study groups. He went on to say that in 1905 Yale University sent more people to the mission field than

---

[117] Ibid., page 32.

ever before. [118]

Georgia- In Atlanta, newspapers reported that 1,000 businessmen had engaged in united intercession for an outpouring of the Holy Spirit. On November 2nd, stores, factories and offices closed at mid-day for prayer; the Supreme Court of Georgia adjourned. According to former Governor W. J. Northen, reporting to the General Assembly of the Presbyterian Church, USA, *"Atlanta was stirred as never before in her history by the simultaneous meetings. I thank God that I have witnessed the greatest revival of my life."* [119]

Kentucky- In Danville, Kentucky, February 1, 1905, all businesses closed voluntarily. Employers and employees marched *en masse* to prayer. The local newspaper declared that *"Danville's day of blessing has come."* [120] In Louisville, by late March of 1905, Henry Clay Morrison, a noted Methodist evangelist, declared, *"The whole city is breathing a spiritual atmosphere. Everywhere, in the shop and store, in*

---

[118] Orr, *The Flaming Tongue*, p. 73. See also, J. Edwin Orr, *"1981 Prayer Series,"* No. 1, *"Prayer And Revival "* Copyright 1994 Campus Crusade For Christ, International, Audio Tape Series.

[119] *Minutes of the General Assembly of the Presbyterian Church in the United States*, New Series, Vol. V, No. 2, 1905, Proceedings of the 117th General Assembly, 1905, Report by the Special Committee on Evangelistic Work, page 31.

[120] *Christian Herald*, February 22, 1905, quoted by Orr, *The Flaming Tongue*, p. 74.

the mill and on the street, salvation is the one topic of conversation."[121]

In Paduca the Southern Baptists declared "a great Pentecostal revival within our own bounds". The First Baptist Church of Paduca received over 1,000 new members. Its pastor, Dr. J. J. Cheek died of overwork. The Southern Baptists declared it *"A glorious end to a devoted ministry!"*

New Jersey - In Atlantic City, out of population of 60,000 the local pastors said they knew of only 50 adults who were left unconverted. In Newark pastors reported that *"Pentecost was literally repeated . . . during the height of the revival, with its strange spectacle of spacious churches crowded to overflowing and great processions passing through the streets".* [122]

New York - In Schenectady the various denominations united to fill the Emmanuel Baptist Church in the afternoon with women and the large State Street Methodist Church in the evening with the general public. Between 800 and 1,100 people remained behind nightly as inquirers. The local newspaper, *The Schenectady Gazette*, ran a special column entitled *"Yesterday's Conversions"* announcing who had been converted the previous day. Another column was

---

[121] J. Edwin Orr, *"Spiritual Awakenings of the 20th Century,"* No. 3, *"Revival in America and The Home Countries"* June 20, 1973, Audio Tape Series.

[122] Orr, *The Flaming Tongue*, p. 71.

entitled *"The Power of Prayer"* and discussed what people were praying for. Other articles were *"Great Moral Uplift"* and *"The Fires of Pentecost."* The women of the town went to every tavern in town to hold testimony meetings.

At Calvary Methodist Episcopal Church in New York City on 2 February, 1905 there was a sight never seen before or since. On that Sunday 2,200 attendees crowded the church. 364 were received into membership of whom 286 were new converts. 1,000 people waited behind to take communion. At the Baptist Temple in Brooklyn, Dr. Courtland Meyers gave an invitation and 500 people responded.

The Baptists of New England reported, *"As the new continues to come from the churches the conviction is confirmed that additions to the churches of New England during the month of April were larger than during any one month in many, many years."*[123] There was no organized evangelistic campaign. Every church was full. Ministers who had been convicted by the Holy Spirit now put their lives right with God and began preaching the gospel.

Oregon - A report from Portland declared that *"for three hours a day, business was practically suspended, and from the crowds in the great department stores to the humblest clerk, from bank presidents to bootblacks, all had*

---

[123] Ibid.

abandoned money making for soul saving". [124] Upwards of two hundred major department stores signed an agreement to close between 11 and 2 p.m. to allow their customers and employees to attend prayer meetings.

From Portland, the Reverend E. P. Hill, D.D., reported to the General Assembly of the Presbyterian Church that *"The evangelistic campaign in Portland has far exceeded our most sanguine expectations. We can calmly say that the city has been stirred from centre to circumference. The very air is charged with holy influence, and the effect of this wonderful spiritual upheaval will be felt for a quarter of a century."* [125]

The effects of the Welsh Revival in America in the year 1905 was best summed up by a report from the Methodist Church which declared,

"A great revival is sweeping United States. Its power is felt in every nook and corner of our broad land. The Holy Spirit is convincing the people 'of sin, of righteousness and of judgment to come.' There is manifested a new degree of spiritual power n the churches. Pastors are crying out to God for help, and not a few of them are gratified to find that help right at hand. The regular prayer-meetings and public

---

[124] *Christian Endeavor World*, April 27, 1905, and June 15, 1905, quoted by Orr, *The Flaming Tongue*, p. 80.

[125] *Minutes of the General Assembly of the Presbyterian Church in the United States*, New Series, Vol. V, No. 2, 1905, Proceedings of the 117th General Assembly, 1905, Report by the Special Committee on Evangelistic Work, page 32.

services seem to be surcharged with convicting power, so that cries of penitence and prayers for mercy have been heard in places unused to such demonstrations. " [126]

In the United States, church membership in the seven major Protestant denominations increased by over 2 million in five years, including 870,389 new members in 1906 alone.

Revival In Korea

In the winter of 1907 the Presbyterian missionaries in Korea decided to use the harshest week of the winter for Bible school. It was so successful that they filled the Central Presbyterian Church in Pyongyang with men, and the Southgate Presbyterian Church with women.

This happened in the wake of the Welsh Revival, when the Holy Spirit had swept through the United States and missionaries everywhere were praying for revival on the foreign field. But Korea was regarded as a heathen country. No one was expecting a great outpouring of the Spirit as in Wales.

Graham Lee, an American, was leading a meeting of over 1,500 men. Before getting down to the business of Bible study he called for a brief season of prayer, and asked one man to open and another to close when two or three others had had the opportunity to pray.

---

[126] *Michigan Christian Advocate*, December 9, 1905, quoted in Orr, *The Flaming Tongue*, p. 81.

But by the time the first man had finished praying there were six more men standing and waiting to pray. When the second man finished praying there were a dozen more men standing to pray, and by the time the third man had prayed, more than twenty men were standing to pray.

After several more men had prayed, Graham Lee interrupted and said, *"Well, apparently you want to pray. Alright then, instead of Bible study we'll have prayer. You may pray."* Immediately, all 1,500 men rose to their feet and began to pray. An eyewitness to the meeting said *"The effect was beyond description - not confusion, but a vast harmony of sound and spirit, like the noise of the surf in an ocean of prayer."* [127] But with the continued prayer came an intense conviction of sin.

An Englishman, Lord William Cecil, was also present. He was so excited and moved by what he witnessed that he did what an Englishman does when he gets excited; he wrote a letter to *The Times* of London, describing the scene:

". . . an elder arose and confessed a grudge against a missionary colleague and asked for forgiveness. The missionary stood to pray but reached only the address to Deity: 'Aboji!' 'Father!' when, with a rush, a power from without seemed to take hold of the meeting. The Europeans described its manifestations as terrifying. Nearly everyone present was seized with the most poignant sense of mental

---

[127] J. Edwin Orr, *Evangelical Awakenings In Eastern Asia* (Bethany Fellowship, Inc.: Minneapolis, 1975), page 28.

anguish; before each one, his sins seemed to be rising in condemnation of his life. Some were springing to their feet, and pleading for an opportunity to relieve their consciences by making their abasement known; and others were silent, but rent with agony, clenching their fists and striking their heads against the ground in the struggle to resist the Power that was forcing them painfully and agonizingly to confess their misdeeds. [128]

The meeting was beyond human control of the missionaries who, horror-struck at some of the sins confessed, could only watch the fire burn. It continued all evening, from eight in the evening until after midnight. Finally, at 2 o'clock in the morning, a lull, perhaps caused by sheer exhaustion, gave the missionaries an opportunity to pronounce a benediction and send everyone home. Next day the missionaries held an emergency meeting, and hopefully concluded that "after the storm comes the calm." But the same thing happened that night, and continued nightly all week long, until the Holy Fire had burned its way through the Church and the body of Christ had been cleansed. In the meetings that followed, conviction of sin and reconciliation of enemies continued. Not only was there deep confession, but also much restitution. The heathen Koreans were astounded and a powerful impulse of evangelism resulted.

That terrible but wonderful meeting was the birth of the Korean Church. In that year of 1907, nine-tenths of all students in Union Christian College in Pyongyang confessed

---

[128] Ibid.

conversion to Christianity in February of 1907. [129]

The Twilight of Revival

As mentioned earlier, the Revival fires sparked by this great outpouring of the Spirit of God, manifesting itself in Revival in Wales, America, India, Africa, Korea and elsewhere, burned and glowed for a decade, until the onslaught of World War I.

With the outbreak of World War I in August of 1914 a way of life passed into the twilight of history, causing Sir Edward Grey to lament that the lights of civilization were going out one by one, not to be lit again in his lifetime. Eighty years later the benefit of hindsight allows us to see such a statement as extreme. But the death of a million men in the Battle of the Somme in France only served to underscore the view that whatever was left of Christian civilization was dying in the trenches of France.

This raises the issue of God's purposes and timing in sending revival. The history of revival suggests that God sends such times of refreshing to His Church, and awakening to the masses, prior to times of national trial and suffering. The Great Awakening of the 1700s preceded the trial of the

---

[129] J. Edwin Orr, *Evangelical Awakenings In Eastern Asia* (Bethany Fellowship, Inc.: Minneapolis, 1975), page 28 - 29. See also J. Edwin Orr, *"1981 Prayer Series,"* No. 1, *"Prayer And Revival "* Copyright 1994 Campus Crusade For Christ, International, Audio Tape Series.

War for Independence. The Wesleyan Revival in England saved England from the bloody excesses of the French Revolution. The American Revival of 1857 preceded the tragedy of the American Civil War. And the Welsh Revival of 1904 preceded by a decade the cataclysm of World War I. Observing this apparent relationship between revival and times of great trial, one historian has commented,

"As we look back over these extra-ordinary religious awakenings which . . . so quickened the churches and so effectively pressed the claims of God upon the consciences of multitudes, we cannot escape the conviction that God in gracious providence was reaping a spiritual harvest before he permitted the outburst of revolutionary forces that have overwhelmed the world, impoverished almost every nation, produced economic and social chaos, and stained with dishonor the pride of Christian civilization. In the history of revivals, it has often been noted that such restoral periods are a warning of, and synchronize with, impending judgment. The harvest is gathered before the field is doomed to death." [130]

As we today pray for revival and times of refreshing from God we must do so with a sober eye upon God's purposes, namely, to renew His Church and to reap a great spiritual harvest of souls in preparation for His judgment

---

[130] F. C. Ottman, *J. Wilbur Chapman* (New York, 1920), page 272.

upon the existing order of our own times. [131]

---

[131] Regarding God's judgment on the current order, the reader may want to see this author's book, *Preparing To Survive The New Age/New World Order*, also available from Preparedness Publications, Inc. or by calling 1-800-879-4214.

Chapter 5 - Revival In America

Chapter 6
Gleanings

A Definition Of Revival

What exactly is a revival? This question must be the starting point for any lessons to be learned from the history of the Great Welsh Revival of 1904. What was it that happened in 1904 that we label as the Great Welsh Revival?

Charles G. Finney was a famous Presbyterian evangelist of the 19th century. His *Lectures On The Revival Of Religion* are classic reading even to this day. But his definition of revival has done much harm, and is contradicted by the historical experience of the Church.

Finney declared that revival in its essence is nothing more than the proper use of the appropriate means. In other words, if the Word is properly preached by the evangelist and the music is properly presented and the right appeal is made to the heart of the sinner, the expected result will be conversion.

Finney's definition of revival has been adopted as the standard definition of revival in modern American evangelical Christianity. As a result, the term revival, today, has come to mean a lively gospel service (or series of meetings), often led by a professional evangelist, accompanied by a talented song leader, where the emphasis of the meeting(s) is the evangelism and conversion of the lost. In effect, Finney and most of the modern church have confused evangelism with revival, and techniques with results.

Re-Defining Revival

I believe that the Welsh Revival of 1904 offers, through practical demonstration, a realistic definition of revival that is valid at all times and in all places. It is a definition with three parts.

Revival is *(1) the outpouring of the Holy Spirit, resulting in (2) the spiritual renewal of the people of God (the "Church") and resulting in (3) the awakening of the masses to conviction, repentance and conversion.*

Lets examine each of these three parts.

1. The Outpouring of the Holy Spirit: Nearly everyone (other than its critics) who saw and experienced the Welsh Revival described it as nothing less than an outpouring of the Holy Spirit upon the Church. But men can neither command nor control the outpouring of the Spirit. That is the sovereign work of God alone. Such an outpouring is usually preceded by earnest prayer on the part of God's people seeking such an outpouring. We have already seen that this was true of the Welsh Revival, which was preceded for several years by prayers for revival and the outpouring of the Spirit.

2. *The Renewal of the Church:* The immediate result of the outpouring of the Holy Spirit was the spiritual renewal of the visible Church. Churches were filled to capacity.

Individuals within the Churches fell under intense conviction of sin leading to confession and repentance. Other believers were overwhelmed with renewed joy and the renewed assurance of God's love and of their own salvation.

Based upon the four points offered by Evan Roberts, believers were confronted with the need to confess their sins, set right wrongs done to others, forsake questionable habits in their lifestyle, obey the promptings of the Holy Spirit, and to publicly confess their faith in Christ. Such obedience on the part of believers can only be described as renewal, caused by the fresh outpourings of the Holy Spirit.

3. The awakening of the Masses: This has to do with evangelism. In the Welsh Revival of 1904 the outpouring of the Holy Spirit had two effects. First, it brought spiritual renewal to the Church. Second, it brought a spiritual awakening to the unbelieving masses which resulted in successful evangelism and a great in-gathering of souls. This was seen not only in Wales, but also in the United States where the Committee on Evangelism of the Presbyterian Church (USA) reported extra-ordinary results to its united campaign of evangelism (other denominations reported similar evangelistic blessing). That successful evangelism should be a result of the outpouring of the Holy Spirit is clearly seen in the Biblical promise of John 16:8, *"And He, when He comes, will convict the world concerning sin, and righteousness, and judgement."*

That the Welsh Revival of 1904 was not primarily an evangelistic campaign is seen in the fact that there was no organized campaign of evangelism, no rented halls, no hired evangelists, and no publicizing of evangelistic meetings. The revival publicized and paid for itself, and evangelism was simply the Divine result of the Word proclaimed by a revived and renewed Church. Denominational evangelists such as Seth Joshua and John Pugh (and many others), who had been faithfully ministering for many years, simply continued their on-going ministries throughout the revival with new and remarkable results.

Perhaps one of the best definitions of true evangelism was offered by the Archbishop of York:

"To evangelize is so to present Jesus Christ in the power of the Holy Spirit that men may come to put their trust in Him as Saviour and to serve Him as Lord in the fellowship of His church and in the vocations of the common life. Archbishop of York, Commission of the Bishop of Canterbury on Evangelism, Church of England, 1945.

Characteristics of Revival

1. Increased prayer and intercession: Historically, revival comes when the people of God are willing to engage in extra-ordinary prayer and intercession, pleading at the Throne of Grace for a fresh outpouring of the Holy Spirit. This was true of the Welsh Revival and its subsequent outbreaks around the world. Unfortunately, much of the current day church renewal movement seems to believe that renewal and revival will come without the church paying the historic price of seeking after God in prayer, fasting and intense longing.

In America one survey has shown that pastors on average pray 22 minutes per day. In mainline churches, it is less than that. In Japan they pray 44 minutes a day, and China 120 minutes a day. It's not surprising that the growth rate of churches in those countries is directly proportional to the amount of time pastors are spending in prayer.

Along this line, I recently heard a well known speaker and pastor in a particular charismatic church renewal movement state, in answer to a question regarding prayer and revival, that *"this time we sang our prayers"* (referring to the amount of singing that takes place in their worship services). The answer, while quaint, ignores the history of revival. No revival in history can claim more spirit-filled singing than the Welsh Revival, and yet it was preceded by several years of intense prayer, intercession and longing for the out pouring of God's Spirit.

The first necessary condition for the any outpouring of the Holy Spirit seems to be united concerted prayer. English preacher J. Sidlow Baxter, when he was eighty-five years of age, said, *"I have pastored only three churches in my more than sixty years of ministry. We had revival in every one. And not one of them came as a result of my preaching. They came as a result of the membership entering into a covenant to pray until revival came." And it did come, every time.*

In the 1740s, John Erskine of Edinburgh published a

pamphlet encouraging people to pray for Scotland and elsewhere. Over in America, the challenge was picked up by Jonathan Edwards, who wrote a letter in response. But the letter soon became a booklet entitled *"A Humble Attempt To Promote Explicit Agreement And Visible Union Of All God's People In Extra-Ordinary Prayer For The Revival Of Religion And The Extension Of Christ's Kingdom According To Scriptural Promise And Prophecies Concerning The Last Days"*. It wasn't long before The Great Awakening was underway in New England; God's response to men's prayers.

For forty years, John Erskine in Scotland orchestrated what became known later as the *"Concert of Prayer"* through voluminous correspondence around the world. In the face of apparent social and moral deterioration, he persisted. And then the Lord of the universe stepped in and took over. On Christmas Day 1781, at St. Just Church In Cornwall, at 3.00 a.m., intercessors met to sing and pray. The heavens opened at last and they knew it. They prayed through until 9:00 a.m. and regathered on Christmas evening. Throughout January and February, the movement continued. By March 1782 they were praying until midnight. No significant preachers were involved - just people praying and the Holy Spirit responding. Two years later in 1784, when 83-year old John Wesley visited that area he wrote, *"This country is all on fire and the flame is spreading from village to village."*

The Awakening of 1857 began in earnest with the Fulton Street Prayer Meetings. In the early 1900s, according to James A. Stewart there were at least forty thousand earnest believers seeking God in prayer for revival before 1904.

Matthew Henry, the great Bible Commentator suggested that *"When God intends great mercy for His people, He first sets them a 'praying."* Dr. A.T. Pierson, the great 19th century mission strategist once declared that, *"There has never been a revival in any country or locality that did not begin in united prayer."*

Perhaps the greatest lesson here is that, like the Disciples waiting and praying in the upper room on the day of Pentecost, the outpouring of the Holy Spirit in revival power comes to a church that is seeking, longing and waiting for Him in prayer.

2. Outpouring of the Holy Spirit in unusual power, resulting in an overwhelming sense of the presence of God and the deep conviction of sin, confession of sin, and desire to make restitution.

At the beginning of the Welsh Revival, Evan Roberts said that there were four necessary conditions for the outbreak of revival. The first of these four points was, *"You must confess any known sin to God; and put any wrong done to man right."*

Confession of personal sin was at the center of the Welsh Revival. In the time leading up to and continuing into a time of revival, individuals are confronted with a deep sense of conviction of personal sin. Why is this? Revival, whether in the life of an individual, or in the life of a church, is a time of the out pouring of the Holy Spirit and He is a Spirit of Holiness. No sin dwells in Him.

As we draw closer to the holiness of God we become more acutely aware of our own sin. We often believe that "sin forgotten" is "sin forgiven". This is not true. Then, suddenly, during a time of renewal and revival Christians are deeply convicted of sins they have forgotten, hidden or otherwise refused to deal with, resulting in confession, cleansing, and renewed fellowship with God. Unbelievers are convicted of sin and judgment and are challenged to confess their sin and profess faith in Christ as Saviour.

This helps explain some of the extra-ordinary phenomena which occur during a revival. Men and women who have not dealt with sin in their lives are suddenly overwhelmed with God's glory and their own sinfulness. The burden of their sin is often crushing, and the release they experience upon the realization of their forgiveness and the finding of their "first love" is exhilarating. At times it is positively overwhelming.

We live in an age where people are told by popular psychology to "get in touch" with their feelings. But God wants us to get in touch with our sins, acknowledge them for what they are, and confess them before Him, seeking His forgiveness in Christ. He can't forgive our feelings, but he can and will forgive our sins as we acknowledge them, confess them and forsake them before His Throne of Grace. We must confess our sin before God and be cleansed by the blood of Jesus if we are to continue on in our pursuit of God. Let me offer a few simple principles:

First, the promise of Scripture is clear that, *"If we*

confess our sins, He is faithful and righteous to forgive us our sins and to cleanse us from all unrighteousness" (1 John 1:9). If we claim this promise and confess our sins as the Holy Spirit convicts us, we will continue to grow and our personal revival will proceed.

Second, Scripture warns us that *"if we say we have no sin, we are deceiving ourselves and the truth is not in us"* (1 John 1:8). If we refuse to acknowledge and confess our sin when the Holy Spirit convicts us, our growth in revival will stop at that particular point, until we are willing to obey His promptings to confess and forsake. Sin can take many forms in our lives: thought, word or deed. What sin of thought, word or deed is holding up your spiritual growth and holding back God's blessing in your life?

Third, dealing with sin must be both vertical (before God), and horizontal (before those whom we have wronged). In other words, if our sin has offended others, we must go to that person, ask their forgiveness, and offer to make right what we have done wrong.

But in addition to this, Scripture commands that if you are preparing to worship and remember that your brother has something against you, you must go and seek reconciliation with your brother (Matthew 5:23-24). In other words, we must take the initiative to forgive and seek the forgiveness of those whom we know we have wronged, and those who believe (rightly or wrongly) that we have offended them. This is working out the forgiveness of God horizontally.

Chapter 6 - Gleanings

Fourth, the circle of confession should be limited to the circle of the offense. Sin should only be confessed to those whom it has harmed or who are directly involved in the situation.

3. Outpouring of the Holy Spirit in unusual power, resulting in personal renewal and empowerment. The outpouring of the Holy Spirit in personal renewal can take many forms (not only dramatic manifestations). Evan Roberts' second point is instructive in this regard. He said, *"You must put away any doubtful habit."*

This principle has to do with the visible lifestyle of the Christian. As the Spirit of God works afresh in our lives He may begin to point out areas of our lifestyle that need changing because they are inconsistent with our Christian testimony and witness.

We see this principle being expressed by the Apostle Paul in the Church at Corinth. In 1 Corinthians 10:23 the Apostle Paul says, *"All things are lawful, but not all things are profitable. All things are lawful, but not all things edify."* There are many decisions that a Christian must make every day on matters concerning his or her lifestyle that are not sinful in themselves. The biblical principle given by Paul is the principle of edification: If something in our lifestyle does not edify (i.e., build up) us (or others) in our Christian walk, it should be avoided. If the activity creates doubt in our minds as to God's approval then it is wrong and should be abandoned, as Paul instructs in Romans 14:23, *"But he who doubts is condemned if he eats, because his eating is not from faith; and whatever is not from faith is sin."*

4. *Outpouring of the Holy Spirit in unusual power, resulting in renewed obedience to God's will.* Evan Roberts' third point said, *"You must obey the Holy Spirit promptly."* This speaks to the issue of our obedience in all things.

Revival in the life of an individual or in the life of a Church requires obedience to the leading of the Holy Spirit. For example, if the Holy Spirit prompts someone to pray for revival, but they do not do so, revival might well stop at that point for lack of obedience in prayer. But suppose they do pray for revival. Soon, the Holy Spirit begins to reveal sin in their lives and to convict them of the need to confess the sin and set it right. If the person refuses to obey and acknowledge the sin and deal with it in confession (and restitution, if necessary) revival will stop at that point. Why? New promptings of the Spirit would be meaningless because that person has already chosen not to obey previous promptings. Revival, whether personal or corporate, stops at that point where we refuse to promptly obey the movings of the Holy Spirit. The mark of the Christian is that he or she is obedient to the Holy Spirit, *"For all who are being led by the Spirit of God, these are sons of God"* (Romans 8:14).

5. *Outpouring of the Holy Spirit in unusual power, resulting in extra-ordinary manifestations of the Holy Spirit.* Every revival throughout church history has experienced manifestations of one kind or another and has had to come to terms with them. "Manifestations" of the Holy Spirit often become the controversial "sideshow" of renewal and revival.

Chapter 6 - Gleanings

What exactly are *"manifestations"*? While we cannot treat the subject in any exhaustive way here, a clarifying word is in order. In I Corinthians 12:7 Paul tells the Corinthians that *"to each one is given the manifestation of the Spirit for the common good."* The Greek word for "manifestation" (φανερωσισ) means "visible, manifest". It is the means by which something is made apparent or visible. Hence, a "manifestation" is the means by which the presence and working of the Holy Spirit in an individual's life is made visible or apparent (within the context of the passage, each of the "gifts of the Spirit" is such a manifestation, but this list is not necessarily exhaustive of the concept of "manifestations" of the Spirit). Furthermore Paul states that such manifestations are "for the common good". In other words, their intent is to edify and build up the body by making apparent the reality that God is ministering to His Church.

Because the fires of genuine revival burn with unusual intensity, the danger is that the church may seek to use times of revival, and its associated manifestations, to determine or define its doctrine, rather than using its time-tested doctrine to test the spirits of revival.

This is important because during revival, personal experience, including extra-ordinary manifestations, tends to out-run theological understanding. This becomes particularly true where there is a lack of solid expository biblical teaching.

One of the clear, but often overlooked, lessons of the book of 1 Corinthians is that the exercising of great manifestations of the Spirit is not a mark of true biblical spirituality. The church at Corinth demonstrated and experienced great manifestations, including prophecy and tongues (glossolalia), yet it was the most carnal and rebellious churches (openly challenging Paul's apostolic authority) in the New Testament, with confusion, disobedience, arrogance and gross immorality in its midst.

We must always remember that God can make rocks and stones to sing forth His praises, and donkeys to speak in tongues (He did it to Balaam's donkey, which spoke Hebrew a foreign tongue to a donkey)! This is why the deep conviction of and brokenness over sin is important during times of revival. It is the conviction and confession of sin and subsequent repentance and even restitution that are the biblical marks of true spirituality, not extra-ordinary manifestations.

God's purpose in revival is to renew His church. And His purpose in giftings and manifestations is to empower and equip His church for greater ministry. It is within the context of these twin purposes that manifestations should be evaluated and understood. The challenge of the church is to experience renewal and its accompanying manifestations, and to distinguish between biblical, godly manifestations and false ones, without quenching the Holy Spirit and His working within the church (for example, the admonition against quenching the Holy Spirit in 1 Thessalonians 5:19 appears to be directly related to the next admonition against despising prophetic utterances in 5:20).

6. Emphasis upon musical renewal and creation.

Chapter 6 - Gleanings

Wales has been described as "a land of periodic revivals." In the mid 18th century England and Wales experienced what historians today refer to the Wesleyan Revival. In England it created the legacy of the Wesleyan Methodist Church. In Wales it left two legacies. The first was the Calvinistic Methodist Church. The second was a new Hymnology. Until that time Wales had no hymns. The Wesleyan Revival of the mid-18th century in Wales gave the Welsh church a rich heritage of incomparable hymns which revitalized the religious life of the nation and the church. [132]

The Welsh Revival of 1904 had a similar effect. It revitalized the hymnology of the Church and became known in many quarters as "the singing revival," so profound was the effect of music and singing.

7. Assurance of Salvation leading to evangelistic sharing of personal testimony. Evan Roberts' fourth point is included here, *You must confess your faith in Christ publicly.*

Evangelism, the essence of which is the public confession of Christ and His saving grace in our lives, is more than a mere characteristic of true revival; it is the heart and soul of revival. The events of the Welsh Revival clearly document that the great burden of Evan Roberts and other leaders of the Revival was for the evangelization of the lost. Everything else was secondary. This burden was blessed and rewarded by God in a great harvest of souls which approached

---

[132]See Reverend J. Cynddylan Jones's *"Introduction"* to **The Awakening In Wales** by Jessie Penn-Lewis, page 7.

140

5% of the population of Wales itself.

Why was the public profession of personal faith in Christ important? Because, this is the heart and soul of evangelism, and without it the Church has no proclaimed message and no personal living witness to the saving grace of God in Christ.

When Will Revival Come?

Many Churches today are asking, *"Won't changing our worship service to a more contemporary and lively format bring about revival and the blessing of God?"* No, not necessarily. Indeed, many churches today are moving to a contemporary praise and worship format emphasizing the singing of choruses and featuring worship leaders and contemporary music.

Changing the structure of our worship service is good and necessary, in order to make it more relevant to the times in which we live. More contemporary hymns and praise songs, a striving after musical excellence, along with the use of drama and other media, are good steps towards a more conducive sense of worship, and a more effective presentation of the gospel. But that, in itself, is not revival. The historical fact that spontaneous worship, prayer and singing has played an important role in recent revivals does not mean that doing these things will generate revival. They are the by-product of revival and not the cause. The Holy Spirit doesn't come in revival power only to those churches with a snappier format, trained "worship leaders" and contemporary music.

Chapter 6 - Gleanings

Are There Conditions For Revival?

If true revival is the gracious outpouring by God of the Holy Spirit then there is certainly nothing that men can do to command or control such an outpouring. But are there conditions which God places upon his church before He will send such an outpouring? The history of the Welsh Revival suggests that the answer is "Yes".

The Holy Spirit brings revival and times of spiritual refreshing to Christians, and to Churches, who are willing to pay the price of revival. What price is that? *First*, earnest prayer and seeking after God for revival. This may include seasons of prayer and fasting. *Second*, confession of our sins against God and putting right our grievances against others (or their grievances against us). *Third*, the examination and changing of our personal lifestyles to eliminate those things which hinder either our fellowship with God or our witness to others inside and outside of the Church. *Fourth*, our submission in obedience to the promptings of the Holy Spirit. *Fifth*, our willingness to openly and publicly testify to our faith in Christ as Saviour.

May these "conditions" become the cry and desire of our hearts as we seek God for revival in our own day. And may we pray with the prophet Habakkuk:

> *"O Lord,*
> *Revive Thy work in the midst of the years,*
> *In the midst of the years make it known;*
> *In wrath remember mercy." (Habakkuk 3:2)*

Chapter 7
Beginnings

You cannot experience true spiritual revival until you have entered into a spiritual and real relationship with God, through His Son, Our Lord Jesus Christ. This is called "conversion" and represents the beginning of the Christian spiritual experience. Your author offers the following as a basic description of how one can enter into a personal, spiritual relationship with God (Excerpted from *The Four Spiritual Laws*, by Bill Bright, Copyright 1965, 1994 Campus Crusade For Christ, Inc. Used by permission).

Just as there are physical laws that govern the physical universe, so are there spiritual laws which govern your relationship with God.

LAW ONE. GOD LOVES YOU, AND OFFERS A WONDERFUL PLAN FOR YOUR LIFE.

God's Love. "God so loved the world, that He gave His one and only Son, that whoever believes in Him should not perish, but have eternal life" (John 3:16).

God's Plan. (Christ speaking) "I came that they might have life, and might have it abundantly" (that it might be full and meaningful) (John 10:10).

Why is it that most people are not experiencing the abundant life?

LAW TWO. MAN IS SINFUL AND SEPARATED FROM GOD. THEREFORE, HE CANNOT KNOW AND EXPERIENCE GOD'S LOVE AND PLAN FOR HIS LIFE.

Man Is Sinful. "All have sinned and fall short of the glory of God" (Romans 3:23).

Man was created to have fellowship with God; but, because of his stubborn self-will, he chose to go his own independent way and fellowship with God was broken. This self-will, characterized by an attitude of active rebellion or passive indifference, is evidence of what the Bible calls sin.

Man Is Separated. "For the wages of sin is death" (spiritual separation from God) (Romans 6:23).

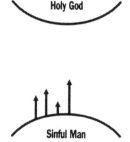

This diagram illustrates that God is holy and man is sinful. A great gulf separates the two. The arrows illustrate that man is continually trying to reach God and the abundant life through his own efforts, such as a good life, philosophy or religion.

The third law explains the only way to bridge this gulf.

LAW THREE. JESUS CHRIST IS GOD'S ONLY PROVISION FOR MAN'S SIN. THROUGH HIM YOU CAN KNOW AND EXPERIENCE GOD'S LOVE AND PLAN FOR YOUR LIFE.

He Died in Our Place. "God demonstrates his own love toward us, in that while we were yet sinners, Christ died for us" (Romans 5:8).

He Rose From the Dead. "Christ died for our sins . . . He was buried . . . He was raised on the third day, according to the Scriptures . . . He appeared to Peter, then to the twelve. After that He appeared to more than five hundred . . ." (I Corinthians 1 5:3-6)

He Is the Only Way to God. "Jesus said to him, 'I am the way, and the truth, and the life; no one comes to the Father, but through Me' " (John 14:6).

This diagram illustrates that God has bridged the gulf which separates us from Him by sending His Son, Jesus Christ, to die on the cross in our place to pay the penalty for our sins.

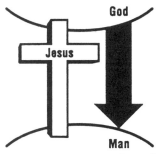

It is not enough just to know these three laws.

LAW FOUR. WE MUST INDIVIDUALLY RECEIVE JESUS CHRIST AS SAVIOR AND LORD; THEN WE CAN KNOW AND EXPERIENCE GOD'S LOVE AND PLAN FOR OUR LIVES.

We Must Receive Christ. "As many as received Him, to them He gave the right to become children of God, even to those who believe in His name" (John 1:12).

We Receive Christ Through Faith. "By grace you have been saved through faith; and that not of yourselves, it is the gift of God; not as a result of works, that no one should boast" (Ephesians 2:8,9).

When We Receive Christ, We Experience a New Birth.(Read John 3: 1 -8).

We Receive Christ by Personal Invitation. (Christ is speaking): "Behold, I stand at the door and knock if any one hears My voice and opens the door, I will come in to him" (Revelation 3:20).

Receiving Christ involves turning to God from self (repentance) and trusting Christ to come into our lives to forgive our sins and to make us the kind of people He wants us to be. Just to agree intellectually that Jesus Christ is the Son of God and that He died on the cross for our sins is not enough. Nor is it enough to have an emotional experience.

Chapter 7 - Beginnings

We receive Jesus Christ by faith, as an act of the will.

These two circles represent two kinds of lives:

Self-Directed Life
S – Self is on the throne
† – Christ is outside the life
● – Interests are directed
by self, often resulting
in discord and
frustration

Christ-Directed Life
† – Christ is in the life
and on the throne
S – Self is yielding to Christ
● – Interests are directed
by Christ, resulting
in harmony with
God's plan

Which circle best represents your life?
Which circle would you like to have represent your life? The
following explains how you can receive Christ.

YOU CAN RECEIVE CHRIST RIGHT NOW BY FAITH THROUGH PRAYER.

Prayer is talking with God. God knows your heart and is not
so concerned with your words as He is with the attitude of
your heart. The following is a suggested prayer:

*"Lord Jesus, I need You. Thank You for dying on the cross for
my sins. I open the door of my life and receive You as my
Savior and Lord. Thank You for forgiving my sins and giving
me eternal life. Take control of the throne of my life. Make me
the kind of person You want me to be."*

Does this prayer express the desire of your heart? If it does,
pray this prayer right now, and Christ will come into your
life, as He promised.

Chapter 7 - Beginnings

Bibliography

Author's Note: The use of footnotes and bibliographies is quickly becoming a lost art today. Footnotes are hidden from view as "Endnotes," safely ensconced at the end of a book where only the stout of heart will bother to search. And bibliographies are either pathetically lacking, or consist of a tediously long list of references, which I can only assume is intended to impress the reader with the notion (probably false) that the writer engaged in voluminous amounts of reading before sitting down in front of his word processor. After all, he read every book in that list, right?

In a break with such scholastic tedium, I offer the following *"Annotated Bibliography"*. It is a short, select list of what I regard as important books and works with my comments regarding the book and its usefulness. I offer this with the idea that our goal should not be to read *"lots"* but to read *"well"*.

Finally, my thanks to the library staff at the National Library of Wales in Aberystwyth, Cardiganshire, Wales. They allowed me great freedom in handling and photocopying books written prior to 1910. By the way, the new library building looks nice, but the old one on the hill overlooking Aberystwyth has that necessary character which makes one feel like a treasurer hunter in search of old and buried treasure. They just don't make 'em like that anymore.

Evans, Eifion. **The Welsh Revival of 1904***. 136 Rosendale Road, London SE 21: Evangelical Press, 1974.* This little book, first published in 1969 and reprinted as a paperback in 1974 is must reading. It was my first literary introduction to

Bibliography

the Welsh Revival. Dr. Evans was of the generation that saw the revival and interviewed many of its participants. Fortunately the book has recently been reprinted by the Evangelical Press of Wales, Bryntirion, Bridgend, Mid Glamorgan, Wales CF31 4DX United Kingdom.

Jones, Brynmor P. **Voices From The Welsh Revival.** *Bryntirion, Bridgend, Mid Glamorgan, CF31 4DX, Wales, United Kingdom: Evangelical Press of Wales, 1995.* This is one of the most valuable recent contributions to the history of the Welsh Revival. It is *"an anthology of testimonies, reports and eyewitness statements from Wales's year of blessing, 1904-1905."* This book deserves to be in the library of any serious student of the Welsh Revival.

Matthews, David. **I Saw The Welsh Revival.** *Chicago: Moody Press, 1951.* This is a valuable work by someone who was there. David Matthews was a music student at the time of the Revival. He was present at the Aberdare and subsequent meetings and records many of the events of the Revival as both a witness and a participant. It was during the Revival that Matthews was, himself, called into full-time Christian work. His observations of Evan Roberts are helpful, and he adds events and details of the Aberdare meetings that are absent from other accounts. Fortunately, this book has been reprinted and is now available from End-Time Handmaidens, Inc., P.O. Box 447, Jasper, Arkansas 72641.

Morgan, J. Vyrnwy. **The Welsh Revival of 1904-5:** *A Retrospect And A Criticism. London: Chapman & Hall Ltd., 1909.* Dr. Morgan was a close friend of Peter Price, the chief critic of the Revival and of Evan Roberts. Hence, his work is somewhat slanted. However, in its essence, Dr. Morgan's criticism of the Revival can best be summarized as "it wasn't the Wesleys". The book is valuable as the observations of a qualified but non-sympathetic historian.

Orr, J. Edwin. Until his home-going, Dr. Orr was the "Dean" of revival scholars. A native Irishman, he traveled, spoke and wrote incessantly on the topic of revival. He met and interviewed Evan Roberts in the early 1930's. He met and interviewed countless other participants of not only the Welsh Revival but revivals all over the world. He possessed three earned doctoral degrees (including UCLA and Oxford), and taught for several years in the School of World Missions at Fuller Seminary in Pasadena, California. He was personally present at Forest Home in 1949 when God greatly blessed and touched a young evangelist (by the name of Billy Graham) and a young businessman with a heart for college students (Bill Bright). His books, most of which are out of print today, are must reading in the history of revival, particularly 20th century revivals. He spoke and lectured extensively for Campus Crusade for Christ, International. Many of his talks were recorded and are now available from the tape ministry of Campus Crusade by calling 1-800-729-4351.

Books

Dr. Orr was a prolific writer, especially on the topic of revival. Here I discuss only those books which bear on the Welsh Revival of 1904 and its aftermath.

Bibliography

The Flaming Tongue: The Impact of Twentieth Century Revivals. Chicago: Moody Press, 1973. Absolute must reading for the history of the Welsh Revival and subsequent 20th century revivals. It is out of print and used copies are hard to find. Orr's ability to find, peruse and quote obscure denominational publications was uncanny, and a challenge to the most dedicated bibliophile! This book is a complete re-work of an earlier book by Orr, privately published, entitled *The Ready Tongue: An Account of the World-Wide Evangelical Awakenings of the Early Twentieth Century.* I found a copy of it in the Fuller Seminary Library. It has some interesting items that did not make it into the Moody Press version.

Evangelical Awakenings In Eastern Asia. Minneapolis: Bethany Fellowship, Inc., 1975. Excellent source on the spread of the Welsh Revival into Asia, including the Korean revivals. Orr once wrote a paper on the growth of the Church in India. He submitted it to an Ecclesiastical friend in the Church of England. When he got no response he called the friend to inquire. His friend responded that he had passed it on to the head of the local university who was so impressed with the paper that the University offered to accept it as a doctoral dissertation!

Tapes

I first heard of the Welsh Revival by means of an audio tape lecture by Dr. Orr. I nearly wore that tape out listening to it over and over. While Dr. Orr was a prolific researcher and writer, he was an even better speaker/story teller, and many of

Bibliography

his personal recollections of revivals and conversations with revival leaders are recorded only on tapes. I only wish that there were more of them.

"1981 Prayer Series," No. 1, *"Prayer And Revival" Copyright 1994 Campus Crusade For Christ, International.* Audio Tape Series available from Integrated Resources, the audio tape ministry of Campus Crusade for Christ International (800)729-4351.

"Spiritual Awakenings of the 20th Century," No. 2, *"The Welsh Revival"* June 19, 1973, Audio Tape Series available from Integrated Resources, the audio tape ministry of Campus Crusade for Christ International (800)729-4351.

"Spiritual Awakenings of the 20th Century," No. 3, *"Revival in America and The Home Countries"* June 20, 1973, Audio Tape Series available from Integrated Resources, the audio tape ministry of Campus Crusade for Christ International (800)729-4351.

Penn-Lewis, Jessie. **The Awakening In Wales.** *10 Marlborough Road, Parkstone, Poole, Dorset BH14 OHJ, England, Overcomer Publications (No date).* Mrs. Penn-Lewis was a recognized leader in the Keswick Movement in Wales and an early enthusiast of the Revival. She and her husband became close friends of Evan Roberts, and it was to their home in Leicester that Roberts retired in April of 1906. This book was written during the heat of the Revival by a participant. Her intent was to demonstrate that the roots of the Revival lay in the Keswick Movement for the deeper spiritual life. This assertion was greatly debated and fairly generally rejected at the time. But her observations are valuable.

Phillips, D. M. **Evan Roberts, The Great Welsh Revivalist And His Work,** *London. Marshall Brothers, Keswick House, Paternoster Row, 1906.* In the years following the Welsh Revival Dr. Phillips became the recognized biographer of Evan Roberts. His work is the standard "reference" work on the life and ministry of Evan Roberts. No study of the Welsh Revival could be complete without a reading of this important work. It is written sympathetically, but with an attention to detail, including copies of Roberts' private correspondence and even samples of Roberts' poetry and miscellaneous "sayings". Although revised in 1926, I utilized the 1906 edition which was available to me at the National Library in Aberystwyth.

Stead, W.T. *"The Revival In The West,"* in **The Revival of 1905,** *3, Whitefriars Street, Fleet Street, London: The Review of Reviews Publishing Office, 1905.* When the Welsh Revival broke out W.T. Stead was a respected London journalist. Stead was himself a child of the 1859 Revival. He traveled to Wales and visited the revival centers, attended meetings and extensively interviewed Evan Roberts. His sympathetic and insightful articles appeared in a number of secular and denominational publications and served to explain and popularize the Revival throughout England. A grateful but saddened nation mourned when Mr. Stead perished on the maiden voyage of the Titanic.

Bibliography

Non-Annotated Bibliography.

Ellis, Robert. *Living Echoes of the Welsh Revival, 1904-5.* London: Delyn Press, 1951.

Holyoak, M. *The Afterglow: Gleanings from the Welsh Revival.* London: Marshall Brothers, 1907.

Jones, R.B. *Rent Heavens.* second edition, London: Pioneer Mission, 1948.

Lewis, H. Elvet. *With Christ Among The Miners.* London: Hodder and Stoughton, 1906.

Rees, J. Tudor. *Evan Roberts, His Life and Work.* London, 1905.

The Story of the Welsh Revival. New York: Fleming H. Revell Company, 1905.

Index